A CLASH OF CULTURES

in Chinua Achebe's *Things Fall Apart*

Emmanuela C. Nwokeke, C.P.

Foreword by Chief Pete Edochie

A Clash of Cultures: in Chinua Achebe's *Things Fall Apart*
Copyright © 2023 Emmanuela C. Nwokeke, C.P.

Produced and printed by Stillwater River Publications.
All rights reserved. Written and produced in the United States of America.
This book may not be reproduced or sold in any form without the expressed,
written permission of the author and publisher.

Visit our website at www.StillwaterPress.com for more information.

First Stillwater River Publications Edition.

ISBN: 978-1-960505-14-9

1 2 3 4 5 6 7 8 9 10
Written by Emmanuela C. Nwokeke, C.P.
Cover & interior book design by Matthew St. Jean.
Image of Ife terracotta bust uploaded by Sailko, CC BY 3.0,
via Wikimedia Commons.
Published by Stillwater River Publications, Pawtucket, RI, USA.

*The views and opinions expressed in this book are solely those of the author
and do not necessarily reflect the views and opinions of the publisher.*

In thanksgiving to God Almighty, this book is dedicated to my beloved Mother, Mrs. Elizabeth Nwokeke, and to my cherished religious family, The Passionist Sisters of St. Paul of the Cross.

Contents

Chapter IV: Interview with Chief Pete Edochie (Okonkwo in the Movie Adaptation of *Things Fall Apart*) on Igbo Culture and *Things Fall Apart*

Foreword

The global appreciation of Chinua Achebe's *Things Fall Apart* is at once a cause for joy and sadness. It is a joy because it is an excellent piece of work that not only entertains and informs, but also presents the depths of the Igbo culture to a global audience. Yet, it is a sadness because it is rare: few scholars or even novelists have delved so deeply into Igbo history and presented it to the world. Many Igbo novelists, old and young alike, have instead woven their stories around the Biafra War. Inadvertently, they have cast a veil over the scenes of the conflict, leaving many to wonder about who the Igbos of earlier times were, and what they did. Therefore, we have Achebe and a few others to thank for what we know, or, at least, what we surmise, about pre-Nigeria Igbos.

I am pleased that this work — *A Clash of Cultures* — is by a rather young Igbo author. It suggests that someone or some people are now daring to peek through the veil cast by the Civil War to see what lies behind. This is very important because, for quite some time, the Igbos have been defined by their angst, or at times outright anger, towards the Nigerian state—in their failed attempt to break away from it. The consequent ostracism hit hard on the tribe's pride and nobility. At some point, survivalism seemed to replace pride, and desperation to have taken the place of nobility—an identity crisis of sorts. But while one man or one generation may adopt different wiles to survive, a mere five decades is scarcely enough to redefine a tribe, or to significantly alter its character, which took hundreds of years to form. For our own good, therefore, the time is always right to dig up our history for survey and representation, in which case, *Achebe's Things Fall Apart* remains essential.

Just like Okonkwo in Achebe's novel, there have always been Igbo men who stand tall in the society—or maybe even in the obscurity of their own homesteads, who believe that any form of compromise is an abomination. Despite their popularity and esteem, the tribe has often bypassed them and adapted to its ever-changing environment. After all, *Igbo enweghi eze* — Igbo has no king. This is most telling in the context of today's pursuit of political consensuses across the world. Peoples of the world are tearing down the hedges which guard their cultural uniqueness in pursuit of advantageous alignments with temporary blocs of relevance in socio-political affairs. For the Igbos, who have no king, it is not in any one man's power to lead such drive for a cross-cultural alignment. It is perhaps true that there is an Okonkwo in every Igbo person unwilling to compromise. Many post-war narratives cloud realizations such as this. If more researchers go behind the curtains to clear the debris obscuring the true identity and history of this ethnicity, they would be doing the Igbo cause great service, just like Emmanuela C. Nwokeke C.P. has done with this excellent piece of work.

It is my conviction that for a scholarly work to truly be considered exemplary, it must not only expand upon existing knowledge but also pave the way for further exploration and investigation. This particular work, which delves into Chinua Achebe's timeless novel, has achieved just that by providing a deeper understanding of our past as Igbos. It is my hope that future writers will continue to build upon this foundation and take us even further. In this age of advanced technology, young researchers and inventors have the potential to make significant strides in the systematic recollection and presentation of Igbo history. With the aid of computers, even relics from medieval times can be made to appear as vivid and lifelike as they would today. By applying the same level of dedication and effort as Achebe did, almost any young person today, armed with modern technology, could accomplish far more in terms of capturing the vividness of their account. It is therefore particularly gratifying to see that young people are taking an interest in the origins of the Igbo people. I find this to be highly commendable and it is with great pleasure that I share these thoughts.

—Chief Pete Edochie (MON)

Acknowledgments

"Give thanks in everything,
This is the will of God for you in Christ Jesus."
(1 Thessalonians 5.18)

I would like to express my gratitude to the team of committed individuals who contributed to the publication of this book. I am highly indebted to my cherished religious family, The Passionist Sisters of St. Paul of the Cross, the General Superior, Rev. Mother Maria D'Alessandro, the Nigerian delegate Superior, Rev. Sr. Juliet Emereonye, and my beloved Sisters of the Guardian Angel Community in Massachusetts, USA, for their tireless effort and support in seeing to the success of this book. My gratitude also goes to Fr. Jude Ali MSP, my spiritual mentor, for his moral support and guidance.

Additionally, I would like to acknowledge my tutor, Professor Davide Del Bello, for his profound insights and direction. Special thanks to the Nigerian actor and Igbo cultural ambassador, Chief Pete Edochie (MON), who graciously accepted to write the foreword to this book and granted me the opportunity to interview him. I am grateful to Fr. Lazarus Onuh, who guided me through the writing of this book and made the process very insightful. To all who contributed to the writing of this book in one way or another, may God bless you.

Finally, to God be the glory for making the publication of this work a reality.

Introduction

The lack of documented records of Igbo culture prior to the 19th century has made it challenging to conduct in-depth studies of Igbo history over the years. Numerous anthropologists have offered a variety of hypotheses in response to the question of where the Igbo people came from. Considering the similitude between the Igbo customs and that of the Jews, some scholars like G. T. Basden, Olaudah Equiano, Dr M. D. W. Jeffreys think on one hand, that the Igbos have connections to Egypt, Yemen, or the Holy Land in the Middle East. Some others like Chief Pete Edochie assert that the Igbos are descendants of Nri, son of Eri, who is himself a descendant of Gad, of Jewish origin. In relation to this, the Igbo oral tradition narrates that Nri is said to have divinely fallen from the sky on this part of the Igboland known as Nri, (a small Igbo town that serves as the headquarters of a priestly cult, with special duties relating to the coronation of kings in the land.)

On the other hand, the Igbo historian, Afigbo E. Adiele, in his *Ropes of Sand,* asserts that the Igbo are a branch of the Negro race. According to him, "available archaeological evidence suggests that this race may have originated in the area along the latitude of Asselar and Khartoum, that is more or less on the northern fringe of the savanna."[1]

However, from the beginning of the study of Igbo history, many scholars had recognized *Nri* as a place of some importance to the

---

1   Afigbo Adiele E., *Ropes of Sand,* (Oxford: Oxford University Press, 1981), 6.

Igbo culture. Indeed, *Nri* plays a significant role in the social, religious, and cosmological systems of the Igbo people and therefore is very relevant in the study of their origin. The above assertion is justified by the Igbo lore and oral traditions collected at Nri in the first decade of the twentieth century. These represent just a part of the valuable materials available for dealing with this question. Since the *Nri* oral tradition constitutes the richest single corpus in Igbo land, *Nri* occupies a place of eminence in Igbo history.

This book discusses aspects of the precolonial Igbo society and culture, from an extensive interview with veteran Nigerian actor and Igbo cultural ambassador, Pete Edochie. It specifically addresses the clash between the two cultures in Chinua Achebe's *Things Fall Apart*, the meeting of the British and Igbo cultures upon the arrival of the British colonialists to South-Eastern Nigeria in the early 19th century.

Several studies in Igbo history, by scholars like Afigbo Adiele, Augustine S. O. Okwu, and Don C. Ohadike, have established that the Igbo people have occupied the current area of land where they are found for over 5000 years. This marks the beginning of the known history of human life in West Africa. As far as history is concerned, the longer a people live in an area, the more difficult it is to unravel their origin. Hence, the antiquity of the Igbo in this region has made it difficult for historians to determine or reach a consensus on their origins. However, most Igbo scholars acknowledge the claim by oral traditions that the earliest settlers in the Igbo region were descendants of the Jews, thereby suggesting that the Igbo people are descendants of *Nri,* son of *Eri.*

Much like other ethnic groups, the Igbos had distinct value systems, traditions, and customs, which distinguished them from other groups in Africa. This is perceptible from Achebe's representation of the British colonial empire in fictional Umuofia — a proud Igbo village in South-Eastern Nigeria. As an African postcolonial writer, Achebe presents viewpoints on precolonial Igbo history and the impact of colonization on the Igbo culture in his famous novel, *Things Fall Apart*. First Published in 1958, Achebe's novel highlights the ruin of his people in the hands of the British Empire with their imposition of colonial rule, and the displacement of the primitive Igbo religion by Christianity. Since Achebe is aware of the drawbacks of the Igbo culture, he was also able to portray the positive influence of British colonial rule on their culture and way of life.

As argued by some scholars like Afigbo and Edochie, the forceful imposition of colonial rule in Igbo land, though harmful in itself, brought institutions and values that positively influenced the society. Although the aforementioned scholars agree that the British colonial rule was a debilitating experience for the Igbo, because of its aims and methods — which occasioned radical changes in the society, they maintain that it did not destroy Igbo identity and cultural soul.

> The Igbo people have remained 'Igbo' in their attitude and style of life. This means that, while changing they were able to preserve their 'ethnic essence' because they were astute enough to use in their own way, the new institutions and values introduced by colonialism[2].

In view of this, it would be the very least misleading to conclude that Igbo culture was annihilated when it encountered British rule. The Igbo resistance to the British led to a series of misunderstandings and clashes, which resulted in the subjugation of the Igbo by the British's dominant power, thus leading to the cultural transformation of the Igbo society, but not the loss of the Igbo culture and tradition.

Things Fall Apart portrays Achebe's assimilation of the concept of conflict as the balancing of multifaceted character traits, that is, of personal and social features. The personal feature centres on

---

2 Afigbo, *Ropes of Sand,* 283.

Okonkwo (the protagonist) with all the flaws of his character, while the social trait centres on an integrated community with its collective aspects. The interaction between the tensions of the personal and social features provides the clash and conflict, which make up the hallmark of drama in the novel.

Things Fall Apart, in a way, demonstrates that any culture or religion that cannot change itself would fall apart with time. Like a living entity, culture is liable to change. The democratic nature of the early Igbo society shows that it was not inferior to the colonizer's; it would have equally evolved and developed into a modern culture in due time if given the opportunity because of the certainty of change. For instance, the Igbos were already producing bronze masks and figurines as a result of their growing technological proficiency in the first millennium. After all, modern European cultures were once undeveloped societies that shared a common ancestry with Africa. As expressed by Joseph Conrad in his fiction, *Heart of Darkness,* (a novel that depicts Western colonialism as a phenomenon that defames not only the lands and people it exploits but also those of the people in the West who advance it) it is this kinship with Africa that unsettles the white man. Hence, Conrad is probably saying that Africa is not the antithesis of Europe or of civilization.

CHAPTER I

The Early Igbo Society

Historical Background

The Igbo people occupy mainly the frontier of the Bight of Biafra in today's Southern Nigeria, with approximately 44 million people living in Nigeria and another million outside the country. The Igbos are one of the most populous ethnic groups in Africa, with a vibrant culture. Precolonial Igbo communities were large, with an estimated population of five to six million as of 1906.

The Igbos did not have a single centralized state. Their political structure evolved around institutions like the Council of Elders, age groups, Councils of Chiefs, secret cults, and associations of women like the association of "umu Ada", (an association of women born to a lineage or town), and "otu umu nwunyedi" (an association of women married to the men of a lineage or town.) Their custom and beliefs were more or less, uniform, though slight differences in language and dialects existed.[3]

---

3 Don C. Ohadike, "Igbo Culture and History." in *Things Fall Apart*. Ibadan: Heinemann, African writers' series, (1996): xxii–xxiii.

Origin

Over the years, a thorough study of Igbo history has been hindered by the unavailability of documented records of their cultural development before the 19th century. The Igbos never had centralized governments nor did they erect any institutions for the preservation and transmission of oral traditions. Among the Igbos, there is a popular aphorism: '*Igbo enwe eze*', which means the Igbos have no king. Hence, in place of any form of central government are varieties of indigenous egalitarian societies presided over by clan chiefs.[4] For this reason, historical records on Igbo culture are gravely limited. Though the British colonists were not so interested in the culture, some of them were able to gather some information about the Igbos. But, with their limited understanding of the culture, it is adequate to say that their accounts of Igbo history have lost enormous value through the years from numerous translations and retelling. The Igbos' lack of a central government presented administrative challenges to the colonialists who, in pursuit of how to rule effectively, did not pay enough attention to the different aspects of the culture. Hence, the Igbo culture that the British knew was the tribe's helplessness and response to the presence of powerful aliens.

Many anthropologists have speculated about the origin of the Igbos. Some believe that their origin can be traced back to the East, to Egypt, Yemen or the Holy Land and that their ancestors migrated from either of the mentioned areas. In fact, some history scholars believe that most West African ethnic nationalities migrated from the East. For instance, the British anthropologist G.T. Basden, in his account of the beliefs and customs of the Igbos in *Among the Ibos of Nigeria,* narrated that "there are certain customs which rather point to Levitic influence at a more or less remote period. This is suggested in the underlying ideas concerning sacrifice and the practice

---

4   Ibid.

of circumcision. The language also bears several interesting parallels with the Hebrew idiom."[5] Hence, Basden proposed that the Igbos were a branch of the Hebrew nation or, at the very least, that their cultural history could be adequately explained in terms of the influence of the Jews. In addition to this, the Igbo writer, *Olaudah Equiano*, in the interesting narrative of his life narrated that

> We practiced circumcision like the Jews and made offerings and feasts on that occasion in the same manner as they did. Like them also, our children were named from some event, some circumstance, or fancied foreboding at the time of their birth. I was named *Olaudah*, which, in our language, signifies vicissitude, or fortune also; one favoured, and having a loud voice and well spoken. I remember we never polluted the name of the object of our adoration; on the contrary, it was always mentioned with the greatest reverence; and we were totally unacquainted with swearing, and all those terms of abuse and reproach which find their way so readily and copiously into the language of more civilized people. (…) the natives of this part of Africa are extremely cleanly. This necessary habit of decency was with us a part of religion, and therefore we had many purifications and washings; indeed almost as many, and used on the same occasions, if my recollection does not fail me, as the Jews. Those that touched the dead at any time were obliged to wash and purify themselves before they could enter a dwelling house.[6]

Some Igbo scholars have argued that their ancestors were Jews and that the terms *Igbo* and *Uburu*—the names of several Igbo towns—are somehow connected to the word *Hebrew*.

Furthermore, the veteran Nigerian actor and Igbo culture

---

5 George T. Basden, *Among the Ibos of Nigeria* (London: Seley, Service and Co. Limited, 1921), 31.
6 Olaudah Equiano, *Olaudah Equiano or Gustavus Vassa, the African,*Vol.1 (London: T. Wilkins, 1789), 30.

ambassador, Pete Edochie, has explained this at length as an Igbo Chief:

> Igbos are the descendants of Eri, as speculated in the Igbo oral tra-
> dition. Archaeological research in Aguleri suggests that we are in a
> sense Israelis; because most of the things the Igbos do, are exactly
> what the Israelites do. For instance, the way we conduct our div-
> ination when we want to contact the spirit of our ancestors, is
> exactly how they do theirs. The practice whereby a man married
> the widow of his late brother originated from there. Circumcision
> after eight days also originated from there. Even the Igbo name Ada
> which is the name of the first daughter in Igbo is also what the Jews
> call their first daughters. We have a lot of things in common and it
> did not happen accidentally. So I am of the opinion that we are all
> descendants of Eri and Eri is one of the descendants of Gad.[7]

However, a central theme in these speculations is that the Igbos are a branch of an African ethnicity. Research has proven that they may have originated from somewhere between Asselar and Khartoum, in the area currently known as Sudan, that is, more or less, on the northern fringe of the Savannah. One possible meaning is that the homeland of the Igbos cannot lie north of this latitude, that is, as far north as Egypt, the Holy Land or Yemen. Therefore, the focus must remain on the area south of this latitude as the cradle land of the Igbos.[8] Archaeological evidence suggests that the Igbos have lived in their present habitat for about two to three millennia before the Christian era. This claim has now been clarified by most linguists who espouse the idea that the Igbo language is a member of the Kwa sub-group of the Niger-Congo family, and that this sub-group's members started diverging from their ancestral root in

---

7 Pete Edochie, "On Igbo Culture and *Things Fall Apart*" interview by Emmanuela C. Nwokeke CP., Enugu, December 5, 2019.

8 Afigbo, *Ropes of Sand*, 6.

the Niger–Benue confluence between 5,000 to 6,000 years ago.[9] Considering the above assertion, Edochie, in a recent interview noted that "archaeological survey has proven that Africa is the original home of man, even though some scholars fail to acknowledge it."

In his anthropological research at Nri, Mr. M. A. Onwuejeogwu came up with the idea that the Igbo culture is one that has already attained maturity rather than one that is still in the process of development. This view is supported by the artistic sophistication of the *Igbo-Ukwu bronzes (Igbo-Ukwu* is notable for three archaeological sites, where excavations have found bronze artifacts from a highly sophisticated bronze metalworking culture dating back to the 9th century AD, centuries before other known bronzes of the region. They include a small staff, a head of a ram, a large manilla, an intricately designed crescent-shaped vessel and a small pendant in the shape of a local chief's head with scarification (*ichi*) marks on the face.[10]). The study of these bronzes suggests a level of culture that would require about a millennium or more years to evolve in an agricultural community not prone to change.

Right from the early days of their exploration of the Igbo land, the British recognized in *Nri* a place of some importance to the Igbo culture. Indeed, *Nri* plays a significant role in the social, religious and cosmological systems of the Igbo people and therefore is very relevant in the study of their origin. The above assertion is justified by the Igbo lore and oral traditions collected at Nri in the first decade of the twentieth century. These represent just a part of the valuable materials available for dealing with this question. Since the Nri oral tradition constitutes the richest single corpus in Igbo land, *Nri* occupies a place of eminence in Igbo history.

According to *Nri* oral tradition, when *Eri* (the father of *Nri*) came

---

9 Ibid, 6.
10 Alice Apley "Igbo—Ukwu (ca. 9th century)". *Heilbrunn Timeline of Art History*. Metropolitan Museum of Art. (October, 2001).

down from the sky, he sat on an anthill because the land was sub-
merged. *Eri* complained about the waterlogged land and *Chukwu*
(a supreme being) sent an *Awka* blacksmith with his bellows, fire
and charcoal to dry up the land. *Eri* afterwards rewarded the *Awka*
blacksmith with an *ofo,* which conferred on him special claims to
the smithing profession. While *Eri* lived, *Chukwu* fed him and his
people on a substance from the interior part of the sky. Eri and his
people did not sleep throughout this period. But when this special
food from heaven ceased after the death of *Eri, Nri,* his first son,
complained to *Chukwu* who ordered him to kill and bury in separate graves his first son and first daughter. After much hesitation,
Nri complied with the order and, after three Igbo market weeks (*izu
ato*) yam grew from the grave of his son and cocoyam from that of
his daughter. Nri and his people ate from it and slept for the first
time. Later on, *Nri* killed a male and a female slave, burying them
separately. Again, after three market weeks, an oil palm sprang from
the grave of the male slave while a breadfruit tree sprang from that
of the female slave. With the new food supply, *Nri* and his people
prospered. *Chukwu* then asked *Nri* to distribute the new food items
to all the people but *Nri* refused because he had bought them at a
high cost — with the lives of his own children and slaves. Eventually,
Chukwu and *Nri* made a bargain: For agreeing to distribute the food
to all the people, *Nri* got a number of rights over the surrounding
people. Which included the right of cleansing every town of an
abomination (*nso*) or breach, and of crowning kings and priests at
Aguleri.[11]

This oral myth establishes the Igbo people's belief in a supreme
god to whom they owe their existence. For this reason, every Igbo
man believes his *Chi,* a supreme being, has a hand in his life, and is
at the same time, responsible for everything they go through in life.

---

11 Afigbo, *Ropes of Sand,* 41-42.

Since he alone determines their destiny, they are ever ready to offer sacrifices of appeasement in his honour.

The story above explains much about the Igbo culture and tradition with the following highlights:

- It points to the importance of ironworks in shaping the nature and culture of the Igbo society.
- It portrays the origin of agriculture and its relevance in the Igbo society.
- It shows the antiquity of the idea of family in the culture.

It is important to note that the story suggests that the Igbo people have lived in their present locality for a long time, since there was no mention of migrations from distant places, as claimed by some historians. This suggestion has been confirmed by archaeological survey which postulates that most of the material culture of the present-day Igbo people date back to 3,000 to 4,000 years ago.

We also see the origin of the symbolic connection between farm produce and worship in the Igbo custom. Again, it could be deduced that the patriarchal authority of yam, the quasi deification of land as the land goddess (for the fact that it multiplies every single seed or crop put in it) and the central role of *Nri* in Igbo history are all drawn up from the oral tradition above which has been transmitted by the elders and titled men of the land for many years.

In *Things Fall Apart,* Achebe gave a detailed history and way of life of the clans of Umuofia, this typical Igbo precolonial society will be of great help to us in this topic. In this novel, Achebe describes a typical precolonial Igbo culture, where the pursuit of personal achievements and success, hard work and responsibility were the most necessary and essential qualities that men ought to possess. Laziness was despised because it made a man seem like a woman, and no real precolonial Igbo man liked to be regarded as such. Achebe portrayed this sentiment in the character of Uloka, a man much hated by his clansmen for his laziness and improvidence.

Precolonial Igbo

Notwithstanding the slight differences in their ways of speaking the Igbo language, the precolonial Igbo people had a common identity and one basic culture, which was evident in their daily social life and communal lifestyle. As a result of their lack of a centralized political structure, they lived in independent villages and towns ruled by their elders and titled men. The autonomous communities were organized according to their line of descent, and these communities were very autonomous in nature. In addition, respect for the elders and chiefs was sacrosanct; the entire clans regarded them as ancestral representatives and, therefore, the wise ones who approached and received word from the oracle about the fate of the land at any given moment.

Regarding socio-political institutions, the Igbo community evolved around the title system and secret cults. In a democratic atmosphere, the Council of Elders' meetings were to tackle every issue that arose in the clan, especially matters affecting lineage members. It was their responsibility to convene the gathering of *Umunna (clan)* at any given occasion.[12] In these gatherings, important decisions concerning the clan were taken. Every member of the clan had a right to air their opinion, after which, with the help of the elders, a concordance was reached in view of what was considered best for the clan on the issue at hand. What is most important is that the elders never made decisions without the consent of the other members of the clan. This suggests how democratic the Igbos were before the arrival of the often-referenced European civilization and democracy.

---

12 Don C. Ohadike, *Igbo Culture and History* (Ibadan: Heinemann, African writers' series, 1996), xxiii.

Any matter that the council of elders was unable to deal with was left to the spirits of the ancestors through the members of the secret cults. More or less, the secret cults represented the judicial arm of the government. They adjudicated and settled disputes in their respective clans. In *Things Fall Apart*, Achebe illustrated the important role of the secret cults in maintaining law and order across the land. The *Egwugwu* was one of the famous secret cults of the precolonial Igbos, seen as the spirit of the ancestors. Each clan had its own *Egwugwu*, who represented them in social gatherings. The leading *Egwugwu* was called '*Evil Forest*' and was the highest among them all. Achebe made an excellent illustration of this in the settlement of a dispute between the Uzowulu and the Odukwe families with the decision of the *Evil Forest*: "We have heard both sides of the case, our duty is not to blame this man or to praise that, but to settle the dispute." Right from precolonial times, the Igbo communities were very famous for their peace-making and festivities in which they celebrated different gods. No Igbo man was to do harm or wish evil on any member of the clan, otherwise he procured the wrath of the gods. *Olaudah Equiano* explained the beauty surrounding the Igbo community thus:

Our land is uncommonly rich and fruitful, and produces all kinds of vegetables in great abundance. We have plenty of Indian corn, and vast quantities of cotton and tobacco. Our pineapples grow without culture; they are about the size of the largest sugar loaf, and finely flavoured. We have also spices of different kinds, particularly pepper, and a variety of delicious fruits which I have never seen in Europe, together with gums of various kinds, and honey in abundance. All our industry is exerted to improve those blessings of nature. Agriculture is our chief employment, and everyone, even the children and women, are engaged in it. Thus, we are all habituated to labour from our earliest years. Everyone contributes something to the common stock, and as we are unacquainted with idleness, we have no beggars. The benefits of such a mode of living are obvious.[13]

Religion

Religion has for centuries been an integral part of the Igbo culture, to the extent that there was no significant difference between the secular and the religious lives. The pre-colonial Igbos believed in and worshiped their most revered god — *Chi-ukwu* (or *Chukwu*), a supreme being, whom they believed was the author of life. They believed in life after death and, similarly, in reincarnation. The belief was that dead relatives reincarnated back to their families in due course. For them, *Chukwu-okike* was the creator of heaven and earth and everything that existed in them. Everyone had a personal *Chi* that played a particular role in their lives, and determined their fate and destiny. Other than *Chukwu*, the Igbos also worshiped other gods like *Ala* or *Ani*, the earth goddess, who regulated all land related issues and, in a way, regulated man too.

The Igbo belief was that the goddess of the land allotted lands to them. It is for this reason that land is considered sacred in Igboland. Hence, the custom of *nso ala* or purification ceremony was meant to cleanse them from offenses committed against the goddess of the land. It is also for the same reason that precolonial Igbos offered drinks to the land goddess, to *agbala* (the god of the hills and caves), and *Ifejioku* (the yam god), before proceedings of any assembly or gathering. Considering the oral tradition about the origin of the Igbos, of a god, *Chukwu,* who created everything and demanded obedience, religion was always a part of the Igbo social life. The Igbos were deeply religious. In spite of the belief that their *chi* had a hand in their destiny, they believed that collaboration with their personal *chi* was necessary for the attainment of their goals in life.

---

13 Equiano, *Olaudah Equiano or Gustavus Vassa, the African*, 20.

For instance, *Nri,* the Igbo progenitor according to oral tradition, collaborated with his *chi* to attain his goals. For this reason, the Igbos have this proverb '*Onye kwe chi ya ekwe*' (if a man says yes, his *chi* also says yes).[14]

Hard work was the very essence of every man, as no Igbo man ever sat reluctantly with folded arms waiting for food to fall from the sky. The Igbos believed in striving for greater heights. This was the reason behind the derogation of Uloka on the one hand, and the toleration of Okonkwo's excesses on the other hand, in Umuofia. Since it was *Chukwu* who determined the destiny of every individual, the Igbo man attributed every success to God, even at the expense of their own human effort. In this way, if one had an abundant harvest, it meant that his *chi* was good to him, and vice versa. Knowing that their chi played a significant role in what became their fate, every Igbo man tried to live in peace with his personal god in order not to procure his wrath or court misfortune. In the event of a calamity, they were ever ready to abide by whatever the gods prescribed as a remedy, including human sacrifice. For instance, in *Things Fall Apart*, we see Okoli die as a result of his arrogance toward the sacred python. The native converts explained that he fell ill and died the day after he wilfully killed a python that was considered sacred in the land. This explains that the gods were able to fight their own battles. Hence, everyone was careful not to procure the anger of any god by offering prayers and sacrifices to them and living in peace with clan members. They firmly believed that their gods would fight and avenge themselves as in the saying 'vengeance is for God'. It was the duty of the gods to punish offenses or reward good deeds. Thus, the Igbos never took laws in their hands without first consulting the oracle or the spirits of the land. It was for this reason that the people of Umuofia refrained from punishing members of the clan who abandoned their gods to follow the Christian God, even when

---

14 Don C. Ohadike, *Igbo Culture and History*, xxxii.

the Christian converts openly boasted in the village that all gods were dead and impotent and that they were prepared to defy them by burning all their shrines.

The early Igbo communities did not exactly know what *Chukwu* looked like, but they knew he is a spirit and, therefore, those who worshiped him had to do so in spirit. For this reason, they did not have any altars or symbols to represent him, rather, they prayed to him through the spirits and the ancestors of the land. Through the media of spirits and ancestors, they also offered sacrifices to the gods in appeasement for their offenses and those of the entire clan. According to Chief Edochie,

> It is only an Igbo man who picks up kola nut and prays with it. In praying with the kola nut, he reminds God that he is there to worship Him. God created us and therefore we have to glorify His name. That is the essence of the Kola (oji) that the Igbos offer to one another at occasions, as a sign of welcoming the other to one's house and of thanksgiving to God. Hence, the Igbos pray with their kola nuts asking God for their well-being and progress.[15]

Igbo men never began their day or any gathering without offering prayers and sacrifices to the spirits of the clan whom they regarded as messengers of God, and who played important roles in the affairs of men. Consider that, in *Things Fall Apart*, Okonkwo, like every other man in Umuofia, had, near his barn, a small shrine 'where he kept the wooden symbols of his personal god and his ancestral spirits. He worshiped them with sacrifices of kola nut, food, and palm wine; and offered prayers to them on behalf of himself, his three wives, and eight children.' *(Things Fall Apart,* 11)

According to Igbo traditional religion, with Chukwu-okike on one side of the divide, there was *ekwensu,* the equivalent of Satan, on

---

15 Edochie, interview.

the other. The Igbos believed *ekwensu* to be evil and contrary to the supreme being, and that his primary occupation was to lead people astray.

Ultimately, the Igbo traditional religion revolved around birth, death, and reincarnation. It was believed that, when elders died, their spirits did not go away; they roamed unseen, looking after the welfare of the living members of the lineage. It was for this reason that an elder would pour libation to his departed forebears before drinking his palm wine. He would also give a piece of kola nut in their name as he asked for their protection and guidance, and offer animal sacrifices in their names.[16] This belief is given further substance in Igbo names like *Nnamdi* (my father lives), and *Nnenna* or *Nnanna*, referring to the return of one's late parents or grandparents. Another aspect of reincarnation in Igbo religion was the belief in *ogbanje*, something that returns or one who comes and goes. *Ogbanje* children were believed to be reincarnated spirit babies who chose to incessantly torment their mothers with the high emotions of birth, quickly followed by the deep pains of death and loss. These children, once they were born, kept alternating between life and death, tormenting their parents. This solidified the precolonial Igbos' belief that death was not the end of a person; that people had the capacity to come back to life after death.

Occupation

The story of the origin of the Igbo points to the importance of agriculture in the life of the community. Everyone, men, women, and even children were engaged in it. Children were taught early how to farm and to work hard. They were taught that the survival of the families they would raise as men would depend on their hard work and physical abilities. The Igbos had a rich agricultural system

16 Ohadike, *Igbo Culture and History*, xxxv–xxvi.

based on shifting cultivation. It meant that an area of land was cultivated for a period and then left alone to regenerate while a new fertile area was sought. This system implied that constant forays were made into forests in search of fertile lands. Success at finding new lands, in de-foresting them, and in the eventually farming on them, required strength and hard work. For precolonial Igbos, the size of a man's barn and the number of wives he had determined his worth and, consequently, respect in the clan. Hardworking men were respected and held in high esteem across clans. And they were highly desired as husbands by the young maidens.

Since farming was the chief occupation and primary source of income for every family, the size of each family's workforce was crucial in the pursuit of bountiful harvests. Therefore, to increase the human capital of their households, men were encouraged to marry as many wives as they could and bear as many children as they could. This influenced the structure and constitution of Igbo families; it promoted polygamy and encouraged a high birth rate as avenues for the desired expansion of households. The major crops cultivated by precolonial Igbos were yam (the staple food of the Igbos) and palm oil. These were mostly cultivated by men. Cocoyam and cassava were considered crops for women.

Another known occupation of the Igbos was ironworks. Archaeological evidence and oral tradition suggest that the Igbos have used forged iron for centuries. The *Awka* blacksmith that dried up the land at the command of *Chukwu* alludes to the importance and the antiquity of ironworks among the Igbos. The ancient ironworks settlement was said to have been located at Nsukka, (an Igbo town in Enugu State, Nigeria) where smelting was carried on in a furnace. As time passed, the Igbos gradually improved their primitive techniques. They began to produce sophisticated metalworks such as arrowheads, hammers, swords, spearheads, bracelets, earrings, hoes, knives, pots, and lots of others. By the first millennium, they had already developed their technological capabilities to the point where they could make bronze figurines and masks.

The third known occupation of precolonial Igbos was trading, which was a subsidiary of farming. Since every family had their own land inherited from their ancestors and had to farm these lands to feed themselves, trade was not very prevalent in early Igbo society as was farming. This, notwithstanding, early Igbo communities were known for their trading skills, arising from the need to exchange farm produce. Their trading expertise was evident in their early encounters with the British imperial government. This perhaps explains why the colonizers initially penetrated the Igbo land through trade routes, with their interest in palm oil and other resources.

Through the various occupations of the early Igbos, hard work remained a central principle. In *Things Fall Apart*, Achebe presented the essence of hard work in the daily life of Umuofia; to the extent that he painted a picture of the protagonist, Okonkwo, as a man obsessed with the fear of laziness.

The development of agriculture and the invention of ironworks paved the way for an increase in the supply of food and mastery of food production systems. With the abundance of food and the constant need for more agricultural investments came drastic population growth. As a result, there arose the problem of low land density and the progressive decrease in soil fertility and overutilization of lands. Agricultural productivity began to wane, giving rise to conflicts among clan members in the struggle for limited resources. The mismatch of growth in population and decline in productivity caused the tribe to spread into forests and, eventually, to begin to emigrate. Around the same time, other professions such as blacksmithing, trading, divination, and artisanship began to grow. Oral tradition suggests that diviners stirred an increase in the development of ironworks as they often requested iron goods from their clients as part of ritual offerings to their deities.

With time, a strong network of economic exchange developed amongst the farmers, blacksmiths, diviners, and traders. This economic network made integration possible within the communities and aided long-distance trade. In addition, it also promoted cultural and linguistic similarities as different clans spoke different Igbo dialects. Following the migration wave, the Igbo community gradually grew and expanded. The population continued to increase and to migrate to other places in search of arable lands, hence the postulation that the Igbos are passionate travelers and establishers of new homes outside their home. This sense of adventure persists to this day among the Igbos.

According to Augustine S. O. Okwu, "between 800 and 900 A.D., the people in the *Nri* core area, as a result of increasing population and innate passion for adventure, began to move in the directions of the Anambra and Niger valleys — Nsukka plateau, and across the Niger to today's *Anioma* Igbo areas in search of more productive lands." Okwu also suggests that the movement was generally not a community migration but individual, family, or patri-lineage migrations in search of fertile soils.[17] A series of gradual relay movements and establishments of people marked their movement, from which some groups moved on to other locations while others waited behind and joined the new explorers later. Because of this, the Igbo people consider leaving one's home in search of a new one to be an act of bravery, vision, and independence.

Beliefs and Customs

The Igbos, like many other ethnic groups, had beliefs and customs that distinguished them from others. Every member of the society identified with these beliefs and customs. As mentioned earlier in this

---

17 Augustine S.O. Okwu, *Igbo Culture and the Christian Missions 1857-1957* (New York: University Press of America, 2010), 10.

book, they did not have a centralized system of government, but the clan knew to respect customs that they believed were laid down by the gods of the land. Among these customs were *Igu aha* (naming ceremony of a new-born child), *Omugwo* (celebration of the birth of a child), *Ikwa ozu* (burial ceremony and second burial ritual) and *Imelu Nso* (purification ceremony and re-connection of the community with the gods). These were mostly celebrative and non-religious.

In addition, pre-marital sex was prohibited, and children born out of wedlock were killed. The prohibition of pre-marital sex was intended to promote high morals and reduce sexual promiscuity in a society where marriage was the only means to lineal affiliation and inheritance. In other words, it was an abomination for a young girl to conceive and bear a child *in* her father's house. Every pregnancy was expected to occur after marriage and in a marital home, hence, the patriarchal rejection of 'unwanted' pregnancies and the possibility of driving the women in question out of their fathers' houses.

However, apart from the customs mentioned, the Igbos had some other customs that were highly opposed by the missionaries when they arrived in Igboland. Some include the *osu caste system,* as discussed below; the abandonment of twin babies in the evil forest; the enigma of evil forests itself; the killing of young boys as sacrifices of appeasement to the gods; purification rituals in atonement for offenses against the gods of the land — especially to *Ani* — the goddess of the land; the mutilation of *Ogbanje* children; the traditional marriage rite; the institution of the *Okpara* — first son — as the head of the family (in the absence of the father); and the taking of the *ozo* title. Some of these customs/traditions will be discussed in the following paragraphs.

The Osu Caste System

An osu, or outcast, was a person who was set apart by the entire clan and offered as a victim or sacrifice of atonement to a clan deity.

They were also known as cult slaves. Since the *osus* carried the people's sins, they were thought to be contaminated. By taking the offenses of those who offered them to the deities, they became the potential recipients of the due retribution from the gods. Because of this, they suffered and lived in isolation, far from other clan members, in locations close to the shrines of the deities to whom they were offered. Because they were not among the community's "freeborn," they were denied all social interaction, marriage, and interaction with the freeborn. The freeborn were superior to them. According to oral tradition, the very first *osu* was a freeborn who chose to become the culprit for the people's transgressions against a local deity and, in so doing, diminished himself to the status of the livestock similarly offered to the supernatural. He was presented to the deity as the one bearing the guilt of the people and its consequences. Having been dedicated to a deity, he automatically became its property.[18]

According to some sources, the *osu* caste system can be traced back to the time when Igbo communities were managed by the laws of the earth goddess (*Ala*). For the people's prosperity in the territory that was given to them by *Chukwu*, the Supreme God, the deity known as *Ala* established rules that they were required to follow. To avoid the wrath of the earth deity and to stop the abomination from spreading among the people, those who were found guilty of great abominations were cast out, and were referred to as *osu*. They were either sold into slavery or given to certain deities to be enslaved by them because it was believed that the deities would ask for human sacrifice at certain festivals to clear the land, so the *osus* were reserved for this purpose.

Another view on the history of the *osu* caste system revolves around ostracization. This took place when individuals or groups disobeyed a community's decision or the orders of the king. Their offspring were given the name "*osu*" after they were expelled from the community.[19] One thing was certain, no matter where it came

---

18 Okwu, *Igbo Culture and the Christian Missions,* 60.
19 Ezekwugo, C.M. *Ora-Eri Nnokwa and Nri Dynasty.* (Enugu: Lengon Printers,1987).

from, the osus were not regarded as genuine members of the clan. They were separated from the freeborn and lived far away from the people. They were considered cult slaves or sacred livestock consecrated to the gods. They were burdened with the responsibility of the clan's offense, as defiled victims and recipients of the retribution of the gods.[20] In *Things Fall Apart*, Achebe described the *osu* to one of the Christian converts as "a person dedicated to a god, a thing set apart, a taboo forever, and his children after him. He could neither marry nor be married by the freeborn. He was in fact an outcast, living in a special area of the village, close to the Great shrine. Wherever he went, he carried with him the mark of his forbidden caste — long tangled and dirty hair. A razor was taboo to him. An *osu* could not attend an assembly of the freeborn, and they in turn, could not shelter under his roof. He could not take any of the four titles of the clan, and when he died, he was buried by his kind in the evil forest."

O*sus* were usually marked in the ear with a long deep cut for easy identification. Thus, they were easily identifiable for the social stigma and derision that was their due. They were not allowed to attend the same schools (as at the arrival of the Christian missionaries) with the freeborn. In addition, they were not given normal burial rites like other members of the clan. In some areas, it was impermissible to bury an o*su* in the same cemetery as the freeborn; they were usually thrown into the evil forest of the deity to which they had been sacrificed by their kind. The *osu* stigma was passed from generation to generation, and there still remain traces to this day. But, thanks to Christianity, the *osu* caste system has largely been erased from Igboland.

The Evil Forest

The *Evil Forest*, also called the "bad bush", was seen as the residence of malevolent spirits. According to Achebe, "every clan and

---

20 "Osu caste system," Wikipedia, last edited October 8, 2022.

village had its evil forest. In them were buried all who died of evil diseases like leprosy and smallpox. They were also dumping sites for the still potent fetishes of great medicine men when they died. An evil forest was, therefore, alive with sinister forces and powers of darkness."[21] Also, in precolonial Igboland, the corpses of all who died 'shameful deaths' or who had traces of misfortune like suicide, were thrown into the *evil forest* for fear they could contaminate the land with misfortunes like death, calamity, or barren farmlands. More so, given that witchcraft and suicide were grave offenses against the land goddess, all who died practicing witchcraft or committed suicide had no place in the earth goddess' abode, hence, they were left unburied in the *evil forest*.

Similarly, the corpses of all who died during the mourning period of a spouse were thrown into the bad bush, since the belief was that their death was provoked or motivated by an exasperated spirit. In addition to the above, in some clans, individuals who were considered worthless, and who did not contribute to the growth of their community in any way, were also dumped in the *evil forest* when they died. People who suffered from dreaded diseases like tuberculosis were taken to the *evil forest* and left in isolation to die. While there, hunger or attacks by wild animals quickened their demise. That is not all; twin babies also ended up in the *evil forest*.

To have twins was considered abominable owing to a belief that a mystical power was behind it. Therefore, twin babies were thrown away to die in the *evil forest*. *Ogbanje* children — who tormented their parents with incessant births and deaths — were also dumped in the *evil forest*. To prevent their reincarnation and return to the clan, their corpses were mutilated before being disposed of.

The arrival of the European missionaries gradually put an end to these practices. When they arrived, it soon became exigent that they needed some plots of land on which to erect a mission house,

---

21 Chinua Achebe, *Things Fall Apart* in "The African Trilogy", (New York: Everyman's Library, 2010), 105.

a school, and health centers, both for the purposes of evangeliza-
tion and the allurement of the 'Natives' who, as it appeared, were
beginning to fancy exposure to Euro-Christian values and Western education. It was also clear that some of the natives found in
the new religion answers to their doubts and disillusionment in the
Igbo religion. Under pressure from the missionaries and the British
administrators, the Igbos agreed to provide land for the missionaries. Consequently, they offered the *evil forest* for the mission house
project. Obviously, they did not expect things to go well for the
missionaries whom they saw as intruders in their land.

It was not the Igbo custom to fight strangers, rather they believed
it was their god's responsibility to fight to protect them and their land.
So, they gave the *evil forest* hoping that the gods, especially of the
evil forest, would deal with the missionaries and eliminate them from
their land. Unfortunately, it was they — the Igbos — that were sur-
prised. The missionaries flourished in the *evil forest*, converting great
numbers to Christian ways and expanding remarkably. With their
gods quiet, the locals came to consider the white man's god as superior. Thus, the sociocultural transformation of the Igbo society began
with the advent of the first Christian missionaries to Igboland in the
mid nineteenth century when the evil forest and all it connoted met
with a mellow but stiff (and eventually victorious) opposition. The
missionaries, along with the British colonial administrators, were able
to weaken the Igbo religion and beliefs, not just by erecting mission buildings in the evil forests, but also by living in them without
any harm from any gods as the natives had anticipated. Before this
time, those who had the unfortunate experience of passing through
the evil forest did so hurriedly and in utmost silence — no one dared
venture into it, and those who were unlucky to pass through it usually underwent purification rituals.[22] While many were converted to

---

22 Njoku, Iheanacho, Onyekwelibe. "The Encounter with "Evil Forest" in Igbo-land", (2017).

Christianity, those who remained adamant merely watched their religious beliefs crumble because of the missionaries' work.

Title System

One of the most popular indigenous traditions and cultural practices of the Igbos was the taking of titles. Among these was the *ozo* title and its variants: *ichie, nze,* and *eze.* Title taking was a social function meant to acknowledge and reward individual achievements. It was a way of enhancing among the members of the community the zeal for upward mobility. Individuals worked hard with a view to improve their social standing and, to be acknowledged as great men of the land. Titled chiefs, in fact, were viewed as the highest members of the clan. They were given privileges in the social life of the community and, sometimes, almost divinized as gods. The main role of title institutions had to do with socialization; they were looked upon by all to instil social order in the community. As respectable elders of the clan, titled men were expected to impress their influence on the community and enhance public regard for the customs of the ancestors.

Therefore, they were like first-class citizens who, with their exemplary way of life, impressed a strong culture of obedience and faithfulness to the gods within the community. In a way, they were the custodians of ancestral symbols, heads of the clan, and representatives of the spirits of the clan. They functioned as the mouthpiece of the oracle, ancestors, and spirits, and were greeted obsequiously with high-sounding salutations whenever they entered social gatherings. At such times, it was common to hear chants of *Igwe!!!* (Sky or His Highness) in recognition of their divine role in the community, almost like gods of the land. Considerably, the Igbos believed that humans were mortal beings, and that no one could inherit immortality or god-ship unless through the *Ozo* title.

In other words, the only way to acquire immortality was by taking a title (*ichi echichi*). In this case, the Igbo word *chi* represented invisible forces, spirits, and personal gods as explained earlier. It was from the word *Chi* that the quasi-divinization of the *ndi ichie* emerged. Therefore, it was only a man with the *ozo* title that could receive such reverence having attained immortality. He was no longer considered an ordinary man but a god. It became his responsibility to lead community festivals like the *New Yam Festivals* and other celebrations. Due to the foregoing, the *ozo* title became the highest and most distinguished title a man could aspire to in his lifetime. Only men took the *ozo* title, women never did; and the men only took it after they must have taken lesser titles such as *ichie*, chief, etc. For each of the lesser titles, there were progressive duties to discharge.

Before conferring the *ozo* title on any man, several factors were considered. For instance, the candidate was expected to be a full adult. He must have accumulated sufficient wealth, possessing barns, wives, and a large household. In addition, his father had to have died and he must have completed the ceremonies connected with the second burial rites of his late father. Being the highest traditional title in the land, no one ever took the *ozo* title while his father lived for fear of usurping the respect bestowed on elders in the society, especially if the candidate's father never took the title himself. As Mahanta and Maut put it in the *Impact of Colonizer on the Colonized*, "no man could attain a status that might equal or exceed his father's while the later was still alive."

The candidate's personal wealth and achievements provided evidence of his hard work and tireless efforts. Generally, those with the *ozo* title were referred to as *Nze*, translated 'living spirit and ancestor'. They were the moral conscience of the Igbo society and therefore they became the communities' adjudicators in times of dispute.

Since titled men were regarded as members of the high social class, Igbo men generally worked hard to attain titles. Men who were unable to take any titles were regarded as 'women' since women did not take titles. Untitled men were considered 'less capable men' who were contributing little or nothing to the growth of the land and did not deserve any acknowledgement or recognition. Unoka, in Achebe's *Things Fall Apart*, was one such man: he had only one wife, was a notorious debtor, and was a lazy man who had no barn of his own.

Asked why title taking remains important in Igbo tradition, Chief Edochie, a titled man himself hence the 'Chief', replied,

> It shows your position in the traditional Igbo society. You take a title, you wear a red cap and there are things you must not do, things you are forbidden to do. There are some aspects of our culture you must defend strongly. That is the essence of title taking in Igbo land, and one is not given a title if there are some pork marks about his origin or something suspicious about his background.[23]

Edochie remarked that he was not given a title because of his good-looking and impressive physical stature, but because his achievements were collated and assessed with the requisite traditional barometers, and he was found worthy. He has accumulated several titles in his time, including *Ozo* as *Ononenyi na Nteje and Agaba Idu* of Aguleri (considered the origin of the Igbo man). He is also the recipient of the Member of the Order of the Niger (MON) award, a national honour bestowed on outstanding Nigerians by the Federal Government and, for his pivotal role in promoting the cause for the canonization of Blessed Michael Iwene Tansi, an honored Nigerian priest.

Speaking on the make-up of present-day Igbo society where titles are being bought with money, Chief Edochie pointed out that there are always two sides to every coin. He noted that before the emergence of contemporary Igbo society, there were people who belonged to dynasties and, in these dynasties, succession was by primogeniture; meaning that only first sons succeeded their forebears.

---

23 Edochie, Interview.

Today, however, people have acquired education and financial resources and have demanded their share from what was once the exclusive preserve of first sons. This development, Edochie noted, was what contaminated the traditional values of the Igbos. For him, it is pertinent to note that most of the earlier custodians of the Igbo tradition, like those who became kings (*ndi Igwe*), did not receive formal education. So, now that most young men have acquired advanced education, they want to debate traditional values and contest traditional positions and titles in their various locations. Edochie acknowledged that it is a good development in a sense, given that education provides a stronger foundation to build lasting institutions. On the flip side, however, he lamented that once people begin to use money to influence traditional outcomes, ancient customs get desecrated. "So it is right to say that money has invaded that part of the culture of titles, but obviously we shall not allow it to die."

The Igbos' Approach to Life with Proverbs

As has been established, the history of the Igbos, at least the part before the dawn of the nineteenth century, is sketchy. The Igbo lexicon and culture, as they exist today, were transmitted orally through the ages. No institutions were set up to document them. Studies have revealed that the Igbo language is a part of the Kwa sub-group of the Niger-Congo family. Only recently, some scholars came across scripts which they have successfully traced back to primitive Igbo secret societies. These scripts, like the *Aro* secret society inscription, have coded symbols of the society. Therefore, offer clues on how primitive Igbos related with and spoke to each other.

It is worth considering that the early Igbo community were unaware of the existence of other cultures, they saw no need in documenting the tenets of their culture for reference or distinction from others. Save for a few inscriptions made by the secret societies, whose members used coded language for themselves only, no other documents from that time have been found. Admittedly, it was the norm in pre-colonial Igbo tradition for information to be transmitted orally. In any case, in the absence of any form of writing and a coordinated educational system, learning was mostly made up of oral traditions like recitation and narration.

Within the oral tradition of the pre-colonial Igbo society lay an artistic framework of proverbs. Deeply meaningful proverbs and folklore were employed to shorten speeches and accelerate understanding. Since the tribe did not know what it meant to write, oratorial showmanship formed out of how uniquely and eloquently certain persons communicated. These persons enriched the Igbo language with proverbs. However, no specific persons or orators were credited with the origination of these proverbs. They were considered to have emerged from lived experiences and the attentive observation of nature.

According to the Cambridge English Dictionary, a proverb is "a short statement, usually known by many people for a long time, that gives advice or expresses some common truth." In *Things Fall Apart*, Achebe explained how the art of conversation was regarded highly among the Igbos. He described proverbs as "the palm-oil with which words are eaten." It can also be defined as short and common statements used by certain groups of people to teach and convey their cultural principles as they relate to what is right or wrong. Proverbs are usually condensed but memorable sayings.

From the beginning of his novel, Achebe remarked that the use of proverbs remains very important in conversations among Igbo people, as they see them to be coming from a fountain of wisdom and respect. A man's use of proverbs in his speech was an indication that he was one of the great men of the land. In fact, Achebe illustrated how important proverbs are by demonstrating that they were (and still are) incorporated into every Igbo person as can be seen in every character in *Things Fall Apart*. Achebe holds that storytelling, fables, folktales, proverbs, and myths enriched the Igbo culture and enhanced its linguistic appeal.

Consequently, the Igbos are generally good orators by virtue of their inherited persuasive oral tradition. This is still visible today for an average Igbo person's speech is colored with proverbs. Proverbs encode wisdom and play a significant role in the social life of the Igbos. Wise men are usually known for their frequent use of proverbs. They tend to say little, and aim at making a quicker impact on their interlocutors through their deft usage of proverbs. In addition, the use of proverbs tends to make speeches polite and generally less confrontational. It promotes pragmatism and wholesome conversations between partners.

For instance, Achebe's *Things Fall Apart* presented a scene where Okoye and Unoka were to settle a debt. Okoye appeared quite polite and indirect in relating the purpose of his visit to Unoka who, upon decoding the wisdom in Okoye's speech, was able to understand the real reason behind the visit. When Achebe described proverbs as the palm oil with which words are eaten, he was pointing to the vital role they play in the Igbo language. His allusion to palm oil is significant, because palm oil was (and still is) a staple ingredient in every Igbo cuisine. Just as Igbo people do not cook without palm oil, Achebe supposes that they do not also converse without proverbs. Their use of proverbs portrays the Igbo philosophy of life. Achebe employed the Igbo proverbs throughout his novel. For instance, Unoka responded to Okoye's visit with a proverb saying that "our elders say that the sun will shine on those who stand before it shines on those who kneel under them." With this, he communicated to Okoye that he would first pay his enormous debts before paying him. Other examples can be seen in the novel on different occasions. Like when Okonkwo visited Nwakibie, one of the wealthy men in the clan, he opened his discussion with a proverb in respect to him: "let the kite perch and let the eagle perch too. If one says no to the other, let his wing break." This refers to the Igbo attitude of living in peace with one another, leaving room for greatness for all, and wishing good to themselves. Again, "As our people say, a man who pays respect to the great paves the way for his own greatness. I have come to pay you respects and ask a favor." Okonkwo acknowledges the greatness of Nwakibie with this proverb and shows how much respect is valued among the Igbos.

CHAPTER II

British Colonial Administration in Igboland

The British Empire in Igboland[24]

The British conquest of Igboland began around the year 1900. Before this time, however, there were already some veiled imperial forays. First was the 1879 establishment of the United African Company — later renamed the Royal Niger Company — in the heart of Igboland. The Company controlled commerce between the Igbos and the British. And when the British declared in June 1885 that the Niger Districts had been under the protection of the Britannic Majesty, they employed the Royal Niger Company to execute their business and political interests in the Southern Nigeria Protectorate (Igboland). The company was instrumental in the formation of colonial Nigeria, as it helped the British Empire to gain control over the lower Niger region. Between 1885 and 1899, the company held control of the Niger waterway, a possible link to Onitsha and Asaba, thereby offering the British easy access to these areas. Following the withdrawal of the company's charter in 1900, the colonial regime could already gain access, through the waterway, into the peripheral

---

24 Referring to the area inhabited by the Igbos in South-Eastern Nigeria.

regions of Igboland.[25] Consequently, these areas, Onitsha, Asaba, and Oguta became valuable means of reaching the Igbo interior.

According to most scholars of post-colonial Igbo, the imperial regime's advancement in the Niger District (Igboland) was accomplished not with peace treaties, as claimed by the regime, but mostly by wars; overthrowing Igbo authorities and systems and replacing them with British personnel and governance systems. There were no real peace treaties or negotiations between the two parties. As noted by Afigbo, "the Igbo villages were not invited to negotiate the end in view but, the means to an end already unilaterally decided upon by the British."[26] For nearly a decade before the British penetration of Igboland, the Igbo nation had already been proclaimed subject to the Empire without consultation or approval. According to Afigbo, Sir Ralph Moor in 1901 announced that "the natives must be made to understand that the Government is their master and is determined to establish in and control their country." Hence, from the onset, British policies proved to be an imposition of colonial rule on the natives rather than an agreement between the parties.

Apparently, it was a well-prepared strategy to conquer the Niger District. It appeared to be more of a conquest and law enforcement program than a peaceful negotiation. This is because meaningful negotiation can only take place between two parties who, at the point when negotiations commenced, recognized each other as sovereigns and equals, and as having the right to break off the negotiations or even to refuse to negotiate at all without risking military reproval. As the case may be, there was no such accord between the Igbo and the British colonial government, but what surfaced was the subjection of the natives to the colonialists that saw themselves as their 'masters.' This meant that the Igbo villages were to shelve their ways and wishes and obey British rule, with the implication that they would not have access to any foreign power except

---

25 Ohadike, xliv.
26 Afigbo. *Ropes of Sand*, 286.

through the British. Again, the Igbo judicial institutions were not to exercise any authority over the British subjects and properties, and were to submit to the British authorities any disputes amongst or with neighboring groups. In addition, they had to allow the subjects and citizens of other nations to exchange their goods freely in their territory, and allow Christian missionaries to practice their faith and recruit new members to their religion freely, abolishing every custom and practice that they found to be obnoxious.[27]

The British penetration of Igboland took place on two fronts. First was the Bonny-Opobo front, which brought the colonial regime to the Southern borders of the Igboland; and second was the Cross River linking to Afikpo and Ikwo, the North-Eastern frontier. Gradually, the imperial regime expanded to the entire southern protectorate, establishing political dominion all over Igboland. Their invasion and dominion led to controversies between them and the traditionalist Igbo Chiefs who thought the white man's intrusion of their land an unjust imposition of colonial rule on them.[28] According to studies, the Igbos had an organized system of government before the invasion of the British. They were organized in autonomous groups, hence, the British's attempts to bring them under a single colonial rule encountered many difficulties. It has been established that before the British's incursion, the Igbos were already at their best in trading. In fact, this was where the British's initial attraction to Igboland lay. Their first ever visits were for commerce, between Igbo traders and the British imperialists. Over time, the Igbos began to notice overt dominance tendencies exhibited by the imperialists in their transactions and tried to safeguard their territories, but the Europeans were unstoppable and eventually made brazen advances into Igboland.

However, their plans were not without obstacles. They encountered enormous resistance from the Igbo chiefs, leading to controversies and wars between the two worlds. In precolonial Igboland,

---

27 Afigbo. *Ropes of Sand*, 286-7.
28 Afigbo. *Ropes of Sand*, 288.

one of the most prominent and formidable social groups was that of
the *Aro* traders. Prior to the entry of the British administration into
Igboland, the southern region was economically dominated by *Aro*
traders. They were strong-willed and did not fancy giving up their
precious social status and economic power. Therefore, *Aro* traders
were effectively a stumbling block to the colonial regime's progress, with their vehement opposition to the British leading to the
Aro expedition, popularly known as the Anglo-*Aro* war which lasted
from November 1901 to May 1902.[29] The result was the destruction
of *Aro*. From then onwards, the British administration, in its expan-
sionism, employed military expeditions in pursuit of its political and
imperial interests in Igboland. Their rampage left large scars on Igbo
social life and culture. However, the Igbo society gradually adapted
to the new order and began to dance to the colonial drummer.

Concerning the preceding, three important factors have been
distinguished to have played relevant roles in accelerating the colonial regime in Igboland, namely, the Christian missions and schools,
urbanization and increased travels, and the new economic opportunities created by colonial rule. On close analyses, these factors significantly influenced the social life of the Igbos more than anything else.
The Igbo order steadily faded as the British strengthened their grip
on the land. It was a life-changing experience for the locals who had
never had such unpleasant contact with foreigners theretofore. Nevertheless, in relating to this, Afigbo sustained in *Ropes of Sand* that,

> Though the colonial rule transformed Igbo society in many respects,
> it did not destroy Igbo identity or cultural soul. The Igbo have
> remained 'Igbo' in their attitude to and style of life, that is, while
> changing they were able to preserve their 'ethnic essence' because
> they were astute enough to use in their own way, the new institu-
> tions and values introduced by colonialism.[30]

29 Ohadike, *Igbo Culture and History*, xiv.
30 Afigbo, *Ropes of Sand*, 283.

The Igbos did not simply surrender themselves to the new regime and all that came with it, such as clinics, orphanages, schools and its enticing urban centres; on the contrary, they brought along with them to the urban areas aspects of their culture and tradition and adapted them to their new environment. For instance, those who left the village for urban areas created well-organized lineage associations. People from the same village or clan tended to stick together for mutual encouragement and support when they met in distant lands. Similarly, they tended to settle in the same parts of town, meeting frequently, say, monthly, at rotated venues where they addressed issues of concern to their brotherhood. This explains why, in urban politics, an Igbo person would normally refer to any person from his village group as a 'brother' or a 'sister'.[31] The village-group associations served to protect members and their local customs and pride in urban centres. Therefore, it would be an exaggeration to say that colonial rule destroyed the Igbo culture and identity. Undoubtedly, it transformed the Igbo society, but did not displace the culture because the Igbos succeeded in preserving their ethnic essence and lifestyle.

Following the British conquest of Igboland under the governorship of Sir Frederick Lugard, Southern Nigeria was joined with the Northern Nigeria protectorate to form a single unified colony, which eventually became an independent nation in 1960. This brought the three large ethnic groups (Igbo, Hausa and Yoruba) together as a federation.

Early Christian Missions in Igbo Land

According to oral tradition, prior to the arrival of the Christian missionaries to Southern Nigeria, culture and religion were intertwined

---

31 Afigbo, *Ropes of Sand,* 345.

and inseparable. The Igbos were not merely a religious people; their social life incorporated culture, tradition, and religion in a way that one did not exist without the other. Hence, professions of faith were not required, and praying, and religious activities were not mandatory for everyone. This meant that the Igbos had a broad range of public festivals (the New Yam Festival) with little or no public religious ceremonies. Those who truly practiced religion were diviners, ritual functionaries, inspired seers, and the priests of deities. These were identifiable by the marks of white chalk on their foreheads, eyebrows and arms, as well as their dressing, titles, and the possession of ancestral staffs of office. They communicated with the gods, offered sacrifices, poured libation, consulted the diviners, and possessed real religious staffs and symbols of the ancestors and divinities.[32] Women and children were not usually part of this group and, for the most part, they were not involved in ritual activities. They neither offered libations nor consulted diviners, unless in the case of a violation of cultural taboos whereby it was demanded of them by ritual experts for expiation. Though women were not part of the religious class, they were, nevertheless, expected to respect and live according to the traditions of the land.

Following Jesus Christ's exhortation to all Christians[33] in the Gospel of St. Mark 16:15, to "go out to the whole world and proclaim the gospel to all creation," the first Christian mission to Igboland was established in Onitsha in 1857. This group was led by Reverend John Christopher Taylor (a Sierra Leonean of Igbo origin) of the Church Missionary Society (CMS) under the guidance of Reverend Samuel Ajayi Crowther. Before this time, Taylor and Crowther, together with Simon Jonas, led an expedition on the Niger, which served as the opening of the Christian faith to Igboland, in 1841 and 1854. The pioneer missionaries acknowledged the cultural change in the mission land but did not want to introduce radical and premature

---

32 Okwu, *Igbo Culture and the Christian Missions*, 108.
33 The followers of Jesus Christ.

measures to effect quick transformation. Crowther agreed with them on the need for selective pragmatism for, according to him, they were not to interfere directly with those practices that were allowed by the laws of the country. In the same way, they were not allowed to interfere with laws that were not among those required for salvation and which, according to him, would be abolished by Christianity with time.[34] In this way, they tried not to be hostile to Igbo culture and were not radical in converting the natives. This was made clear in Taylor's words:

> A missionary cannot isolatedly pull down long habits of traditional air handed down to posterity without seriously implicating himself to the politics of the nation — he may warn and lift up his voice against the madness of the people. [...] beyond that, he cannot go, it requires a high hand of authority to subjugate and suppress such inhumanity.[35]

According to Okwu and Afigbo, the Sierra Leone Wesleyan missionary body, among whom were Taylor and his Sierra Leonean colleagues (who were also of Igbo parents), established the first mission in Igboland. They worked hard in the Niger Mission notwithstanding the tough cultural conditions in which they found themselves. The African CMS missionaries were generally educated in Christian training institutions; thus, their education, in a way, compromised their relationship with their indigenous culture for the simple fact that they were raised in cultures different from those of their origin.

Sometime in 1885, European Evangelicals who were driven to make changes contrary to the fruits of the Sierra Leoneans' pragmatism replaced the Sierra Leonean missionaries. In Okwu's words, "the European Evangelical missionaries evidently were 'driven to'

---

34 Okwu, *Igbo Culture and the Christian Missions,* 100.
35 Ibid, 101.

changes that essentially amounted to a renunciation in totality of the structures and systems which the Sierra Leonean missionaries had put in place." The Evangelicals, unlike their predecessors, were so radical that they even wanted to change everything that the Sierra Leoneans labored to build, including time, mode, and the location of places of worship. They wanted to stop Igbo communicants from receiving the Holy Communion, and almost rejected the Christian message of the pioneer missionaries, only failing to do so because it was the same message of Christ.

To portray how revolutionary their mission was, Okwu noted that "one would wonder in the context of the nature and scope of the changes, whether the pioneer missionaries preached and practiced a different brand of Christianity, or whether in fact, they were ever ordained as ministers of the church whose religious message and principles they were chosen to deliver and to establish in Igbo land."[36] From what has been said, we can figure out the level of hostility with which the early European missionaries evangelized in Igboland. They were over-zealous and enthusiastic about reforming the natives and their traditions by introducing reformation ideas and plans that forbade indigenous customs and practices. They did this while disregarding counsel from local church agents who cautioned that the practices they sought to outlaw were neither harmful to Christianity nor had anything to do with pagan rituals. Among the practices that the Evangelicals banned were naming ceremony, payment of bride price, and customary marriage, which all had no evil undertones. These young European missionaries suspended local church missionaries and Christians who appeared to be against their reformatory program and who were involved in any of the indigenous practices they banned. The indigenous Christians, in reaction to the Evangelical missionaries' hostility towards their culture, and in defense of the local missionaries sent away by the European

---

36 Okwu, *Igbo Culture and the Christian Missions,* 101.

missionaries, wrote a letter to the European Teachers expressing their impression that the Evangelicals had come to destroy rather than to build up. With considerable ethnocentric prejudgment on Igbo culture and religion, the missionaries had perceived many aspects of the indigenous people's way of life as fetish and, therefore, valid targets for condemnation.[37]

It is important to note that missionary advancement in Igbo land was inaugurated from three main axes: the River Niger, the Cross River, and the Opobo-Bonny axes. The Niger axis was the earliest to be established by the CMS missionaries in 1857 in Onitsha. However, the early missions in Igboland, made little progress during this period for some reasons. Firstly, the missionaries sought to convert Africans through their kings and chiefs, a strategy unsuitable to Igboland where there were no kings and chiefs powerful enough to drag their people along with them into Christianity. Secondly, the disposition of the Igbos to the white man had, by this time, become complex due to the unfortunate encounters with British colonial rule. When, in 1885, the Catholics, led by the Holy Ghost Fathers, reinforced the Christian mission, the British conquest of Igboland had already taken place. Hence, there was a conversion explosion following the conquest. Many Igbo people began to fancy the missionaries' educative program, their school, and everything that came with their mission.[38]

Unlike in many other parts of Africa, it is important to note that preaching "Christ Crucified" was not so much the incentive for the Christian mission in Igboland as it was the parade of the advantages of literacy over illiteracy, which took place in schools. The school played an important role in the conversion of Igbo people. The missionaries discovered early enough that direct appeal and preaching would not achieve much in terms of converting the Igbos to Christianity in good numbers, so, to succeed, they decided to use

---

37 Ibid.
38 Afigbo. *Ropes of Sand*, 339.

the school as an instrument.[39] Thus, their introduction of the school as a means for conversion became a turning point in the history of Christianity in Igboland. As Kanayo L. Nwadialor & Ikenna L. Umeanolue put it in their historical discourse:

> The missionaries changed indigenous Igbo society much more radically than either the government or the traders did by insisting that the Igbo people and their neighbor could not actually become good Christians or attain salvation unless they modify their societies drastically along prescribed western lines. They offered western education, highly attractive bait which indigenous religion could not offer. Since the Igbo people were anxious to acquire the white man's irresistible magic and knew this could only be done through going to school, they in time sent flocks of their children to the schools, soon, political, economic, religious and social life came to be dominated by the natives who had acquired the white man's magic.[40]

In effect, through the schools, the missionaries leveraged the burning desire of the Igbos who wanted to become like the British in manipulating their physical world. In Afigbo's words, it could be said that "the Igbo were not converted to Christianity, they were ensnared for Christianity by the school." The school played a fundamental role in changing Igbo society because it was the tool for mobilizing support for Christianity and for withdrawing support from the old social order. In addition, the schools helped in producing indigenes who later assisted in spreading the gospel in the local languages among their people. Notably, the early converts consisted of a few slaves, *Osu* (outcasts), and children. This was because the

---

39 Afigbo. *Ropes of Sand*, 339.
40 Kanayo L. Nwadialor & Ikenna L. Umeanolue, "Missionary factor in the making of a Modern Igbo Nation." 1841-1940: *A Historical Discourse,* Vol.1 No. 4, (2012),114, https://www.ajol.info/index.php/jrhr/article/view/86985.

younger generation was not yet fully initiated into the culture, and they had less contact with the indigenous customs as against the elders who already embodied the traditions of their fathers. The fact that the first generation of Igbo Christians had limited contact with their tradition and seemed to be against it facilitated the expansion of the Christian mission in Igboland. This is because, while time and death gradually reduced the number of the defenders of the old order, the number of Christians increased progressively. In addition, many of those who were sent to school first were slaves who, because of their social status, resented the Igbo culture and society. As a result, they saw Christianity as an alternative to the Igbo society and were happy to escape the limitations that the Igbo tradition prescribed for them. Accordingly, Afigbo asserts that,

> The school further dealt severe blows on indigenous Igbo culture not only because it was the instrument through which a large fraction of the younger generation of Igbo men were indoctrinated against the society and its values, but also because it tended to withdraw them physically from participating in those celebrations and social processes by which the values of the group were transmitted from generation to generation.[41]

What happened was that schoolchildren spent most of their day being indoctrinated in school. They left their homes very early in the morning and came back very tired late in the day. They spent their Saturdays doing household chores, and this left them with little or no time to practice indigenous customs. The school's influence on Igbo culture became immediately apparent. The school became an indisputable means of excelling in the new world introduced by colonial rule, as children who had studied under the missionaries gained employment as clerks and messengers within a few years. They

---

41 Afigbo, *Ropes of Sand*, 341.

acquired new economic power and social status and became objects of admiration in the land. On this account, those initially opposed to sending their children to school changed their minds and embraced the white man's school. Consequently, the Igbo community entered a new phase of existence. The two cultures gradually mixed up; the Igbo culture got transformed but was not totally disintegrated.[42]

Christian Missionaries in *Things Fall Apart*

In the Gospel of Mark 16:15, Jesus commanded His disciples to go into the whole world and preach the gospel to every creature. Here, this study will attempt to analyze this exhortation by Christ to His followers. To proceed, it would be interesting first to consider *Pope Pius XI's Encyclical on Catholic Missions* in which he outlined the Church's mission in evangelizing all nations. He writes that "The Church has no other reason for existence than, by developing the Kingdom of Christ on earth, and to make mankind participate in the effects of His saving Redemption."[43] This implies that it is the work of the missionaries to enlighten by faith, all humanity, starting from their lands to other unknown lands at their immediate discovery. This Encyclical required that a much larger number than heretofore of missionaries, well trained in the different fields of knowledge, be sent into the vast regions which are still deprived of the civilizing influence of the Christian religion; and, that the faithful be brought to understand with what zeal, constancy in prayer, and with what generosity they too must cooperate in a work which is so holy and fruitful (art.3). It also emphasized the importance of building up a native clergy to facilitate the mission.

---

42 Ibid, 341.

43 Pope Pius XI, Encyclical on Catholic Missions, *Rerum Ecclesiae* (28 February 1926) §1, at The Holy See, https://www.vatican.va/content/pius-xi/en/encyclicals/documents/hf_p-xi_enc_28021926_rerum-ecclesiae.html.

In this light, the missionaries were required to cooperate with the local faithful in propagating the Christian faith. They had to be well prepared for the tasks of the mission, and ought to have a friendly, welcoming attitude toward the natives. Similarly, an Encyclical of Pope Benedict XV, *Maximum Illud, On the Propagation of the Faith throughout the World,* outlined what ought to be the primary concern of those in charge of Christian missions. Pope Benedict XV points out that:

> The superior of a mission should make it one of his primary con-
> cerns to expand and fully develop his mission. The entire region
> within the boundaries of his mission has been committed to his care;
> He must not consider that he is properly discharging the duties of
> his office unless he is working constantly and with all the vigour he
> can muster to bring the other, far more numerous, inhabitants of the
> area to partake of the Christian truth and the Christian life.[44]

The above is encouraging missionaries to work for a spiritual goal, that their task is a divine one, and that it is far beyond the reach of human reasoning. The pontiff declared that missionaries had been called to carry light to men who lie in the shadow of death and to open the way to heaven for souls that are hurtling toward destruc-tion. In addition, he insists that it would be a tragedy if a missionary were to spend himself in attempts to increase and exalt the prestige of the native land he left behind him, stating that no matter how unsophisticated the people may appear to be, they are always well aware of what the missionary is doing in their country and what he wants for them. If the natives were to find out that the missionary is serving the interest of his homeland, instead of devoting himself exclusively to the work of God, they would acquire the conviction

---

44 Pope Benedict XV, Encyclical on the Propagation of the Faith throughout the World, *Max-imum Illud* (30 November 1919) § 11, at The Holy See, https://www.vatican.va/content/benedict-xv/en/apost_letters/documents/hf_ben-xv_apl_19191130_maximum-illud.html.

that the Christian religion is the national religion of some foreign people and that anyone converted to it is abandoning his loyalty to his own people and submitting to the pretensions and domination of a foreign power (*Maximum Illud*, 1919)

Presumably, the above appeal was made in response to early missionary experiences. In the case of Igboland, the first European missionaries were very hostile to the local culture. Achebe's *Things Fall Apart* reflects this hostility: Firstly, the missionaries' arrival to Umuofia was compared to the arrival of locusts — a presupposition of annihilation in the land. As represented in *Things Fall Apart*, the Igbos could draw parallels between the mission of the colonial government and that of the Christian missionaries. We read in chapter eighteen of the novel that the white man did not only bring his religion with him, but he also brought his government.

> But stories were already gaining ground that the white man had not only brought a religion but also a government. It was said that they had built a place of judgment in Umuofia to protect the followers of their religion. It was even said that they had hanged one man who killed a missionary.[45]

The background and essence of *Maximum Illud*, which urges the missionary to not work as an agent of his native country but as an ambassador of Christ, begins to come into prominence. Per this Encyclical, the British missionaries gave the Igbo natives the wrong impression about missionaries, as they appeared to serve the interests of their homeland by merging the goals of their mission with the goals of British colonial rule. They made Christianity appear as a national religion of the dominating European power, making it difficult for them to work well with the natives. As has been deduced, there were controversies between the missionaries and the men of

---

45 Achebe, *Things Fall Apart*, 109.

Umuofia who had the impression that the white missionaries were working with the colonial regime to supplant their way of life with their national culture and religion. The settlements of the Christian missionaries were guarded and partly run by personnel of the colonial government. For instance, *Things Fall Apart* shows Mr Smith, a missionary, working with the District Commissioner against the indigenous people during conflicts.

Art. 24 of *Maximum Illud* demonstrates that:

> Among the attainments necessary for the life of a missionary, a place of paramount importance must obviously be granted to the language of the people to whose salvation he will devote himself. ....For in this respect he is under an obligation to all those he deals with, the learned and the ignorant alike, and he will soon realize the advantage a command of their language gives him in the task of winning the confidence of the populace. If he is earnest about his work, he will be particularly reluctant to delegate the explanation of Christian doctrine to his catechists. ...There will also be occasions when, in his position as representative and interpreter of our holy Faith, he will have to associate with the dignitaries of the district. Or he may be invited to appear at scholarly gatherings. How will he maintain his dignity under these circumstances if he cannot make himself understood because he does not know the language?[46]

Therefore, in the context of *Things Fall Apart*, the missionaries failed. They paid little or no attention to Igbo culture and were not interested in learning the language. They relied on new converts and catechists for interpretation, thereby delegating their work and mission to others and running the risk of misrepresentation of the gospel. In many cases, their interpreters faltered in the accurate rendition of what they intended to convey to the natives. There was

---

46 Pope Benedict XV, *Maximum Illud,* art.24.

also the challenge of different dialects within the same language. Hence, the Umuofia scene presents the natives making fun of the interpreters who could not communicate effectively in their dialect. On account of this, the core missionary message was sometimes undermined by the missionaries' indifference to Igbo culture and language. Moreover, the novel also presented scenarios where the interpreters served as instruments for fermenting conflicts between the natives and the missionaries. In several ways, therefore, the use of interpreters caused more harm than good in preaching the gospel in Igbo land as noted in chapter sixteen:

> When they had all gathered, the white man began to speak to them. He spoke through an interpreter who was an Ibo man, though his dialect was different and harsh to the ears of Mbanta. Many people laughed at his dialect and the way he used words strangely. Instead of saying 'myself', he always said 'my buttocks.'[47]

Instances abound. In the same chapter, the white man addressed the people thus: "We have been sent by this great God to ask you to leave your wicked ways and false gods and turn to Him so that you may be saved when you die." One of the members of the clan made a joke out of everything that was said, causing a stir in the crowd, deriding and reducing the true message of the gospel:

> Your buttocks understand our language," said someone light-heartedly and the crowd laughed. "What did he say?" the white man asked his interpreter. But before he could answer, another man asked a question: "Where is the white man's horse?" he asked. ...."Tell them," he said, "that I shall bring many iron horses when we have settled down among them. Some of them will even ride the iron horse themselves." This was interpreted to them but very

---

47 Achebe, *Things Fall Apart,* 102.

few of them heard. ….After the singing the interpreter spoke about the Son of God whose name was Jesu Kristi. Okonkwo, who only stayed in the hope that it might come to chasing the men out of the village or whipping them, now said "You told us with your own mouth that there was only one god. Now you talk about his son. He must have a wife, then." The crowd agreed. "I did not say He had a wife," said the interpreter, somewhat lamely. "Your buttocks said he had a son," said the joker. "So he must have a wife and all of them must have buttocks."[48]

Although the missionaries were, in some cases, able to convey their message through interpreters, their preaching of the good news was often jeopardized by the interpreters' carefree approach to interpreting and the natives' light-hearted reception of the message. The natives thought that the white man had indeed brought a lunatic religion to their land. This was so because their messages sometimes lost their true meaning in the mouth of the interpreter, through interpretations, because the interpreter had limited knowledge of either the language of the speaker or that of the audience.

An example of how a message could lose its meaning or take on new meaning is seen in the scene in chapter twenty-two where Mr Smith and members of *Egwugwu* secret society had a confrontation. When Mr Smith said to his interpreter: "Tell them to go away from here. This is the house of God, and I will not live to see it desecrated." Okeke interpreted: "The white man says he is happy you have come to him with your grievances, like friends. He will be happy if you leave the matter in his hands."

Another example can be drawn from the court in the case between the District Commissioner and the arrested elders: "I have decided that you will pay a fine of two hundred bags of cowries. (The shell of a small sea creature with a soft and a brightly coloured

---

48 Ibid, 102.

body, used in the past as money in parts of Africa and southern Asia.) You will be released as soon as you agree to this and undertake to collect that fine from your people." As soon as the six men were locked up, court messengers went into Umuofia to tell the people that their leaders would not be released unless they paid a fine of two hundred and fifty bags of cowries. "Unless you pay the fine immediately," said their headman, "we will take your leaders to Umuru before the big white man, and hang them." Here we see the court messengers twist the message by adding fifty bags of cowries to the original two hundred stipulated by the Commissioner and, in addition, they told the people that their failure to comply would warrant the execution of their elders by hanging, which was not included in the commissioner's message.

The interpreters exploited the white man's linguistic incapacity to manipulate the natives. In chapter twenty, Obierika tells Okonkwo that the land dispute between two clan members had been resolved in favor of the Nnama's family because he had given much money to the white man's messengers and interpreter. In a sense, it seemed as if colonialism birthed bribery and corruption in the Igbo community, as such a thing never existed among the members of the clans.

It could be said, then, that the white man's indifference to Igbo culture resulted in a series of problems between new converts and the clan as we read a conversation between Okonkwo and his friend Obierika: "Does the white man understand our custom about land? How can he when he does not even speak our tongue? But he says that our customs are bad." Deducing from this conversation, it is obvious that the British administrators' indifference was noticed by the natives, and it fuelled their disenchantment with the white man's domineering culture and religion.

St. Paul, a phenomenal teacher and writer, espoused a missionary principle that the missionaries in *Things Fall Apart* failed to carry on, save for Mr Brown, the predecessor of Mr. Smith. For instance,

Art. 24 of *Maximum Illud* piggybacks on St. Paul's first letter to the
Corinthians 9:20-23:

> To the Jews I made myself as a Jew, to win the Jews. To those under
> the law as one under the law (though I myself am not under the
> law), so as to win those under the law. To those not having the law
> as one not having the law (though I am not free from God's law but
> am under Christ's law), so as to win those not having the law. To
> the weak I made myself weak, to win the weak. I accommodated
> myself to people in all kinds of different situations, so that by all
> possible means I might bring some to salvation. All this I do for the
> sake of the gospel, that I may share its benefits with others.[49]

Mr Brown maintained a peaceful relationship between the new
converts and the rest of the clan, as we see in his encounter with
Akunna. Through their conversation, he came to realize that a frontal attack on the native culture would be of no use, and so decided
to make use of the school, which proved to be successful in driving
Christian missionary work home in Igboland.

Mr Brown was quite astute; he avoided any conflict with the
people of Umuofia by frequently employing dialogue, thus he was
successful in converting many to Christianity. He also made the
people understand that his presence was for their own ultimate good.
Mr. Brown preached against overzealousness amongst his converts.

> Everything was possible, he told his energetic flock, but everything
> was not expedient. And so Mr. Brown came to be respected even
> by the clan, because he trod softly on its faith. He made friends with
> some of the great men of the clan and on one of his frequent visits
> to the neighboring villages he had been presented with a carved
> elephant tusk, which was a sign of dignity and rank.[50]

---

49 The New Jerusalem Bible (1 Corinthians 9:20-23).
50 Achebe, *Things Fall Apart,* 126.

However, all he had worked for seemed to crumble upon the arrival of Mr. Smith who condemned his policy of compromise and accommodation. "Mr Smith saw things as black and white and black was evil. He saw the world as a battlefield in which the children of light were locked in mortal conflict with the sons of darkness. He believed in slaying the prophets of Baal." Hence, the mission soon descended into chaos with disputes arising repeatedly between Christians and members of the clan in both parties' quest to preserve their culture and religion.

It is also noteworthy, from *Things Fall Apart*, that the missionaries did not hold any negotiations with the natives. In the case where the commissioner arrested the elders for burning down the Church, he told them that: "We have a court of law where we judge cases and administer justice just as it is done in my own country under a great queen. I have brought you here because you joined together to molest others, to burn people's houses and their places of worship. That must not happen in the dominion of our queen." Here, it must be true that the natives had no idea whatsoever what the commissioner was talking about. They had not been in any negotiations with the British on what laws would apply in their land. They seemed to have been enslaved in their own land by the laws of a queen they didn't even know existed. In fact, Umuofia did not have such a law that forbade the burning of a church. To them, their actions were noble, for they defended their land and culture.

From a moral point of view, the natives were within their rights to resist the British, reject their religion and politics, and even burn down their institutions. Interestingly, where the British might have employed negotiation, it was the natives who made an attempt to negotiate. In the sixteenth chapter of *Things Fall Apart*, a man from Mbanta asked the missionaries, "if we leave our gods and follow your god, who will protect us from the anger of our neglected gods and ancestors?" The white missionary callously replied: "your gods are not alive and cannot do you any harm, they are pieces of wood and stone." Upon hearing this, the men of Mbanta broke into derisive laughter.

It was hilarious to tell a clan that had only known *agbala* (god of the hills and caves) and *ani* (the land goddess) as their gods that these were nothing but pieces of wood. The men could not digest the idea that Ani and Amadiora, Idemili and Ogwugwu were harmless. These missionaries must be mad, they thought, and some of them began to walk away. The thought that the missionaries were mad was indeed the genesis of the conflict that ensued between the white man and the Igbo community.

It can be argued that the Christian mission in Umuofia (Igbo-land) could have fared much better if the missionaries had employed negotiation. Unfortunately, they did the contrary, neglecting the language and culture, and procuring interpreters who, either deliberately or ignorantly, adulterated their message. This clash of cultures has prompted diverse discourse over the years, prompting Pope Pius XII's Encyclical, *Evangelii Praecones,* in 1951. The Encyclical bordered on the promotion of Catholic Missions, stating that:

> In view of the upheavals and dangers of the present time, when not a few peoples are divided by conflicting interests, we consider it very opportune on the present occasion to reiterate our approval of this work. For missionaries to preach to all men the practice of natural and Christian virtues and, that brotherly and common fellowship which transcends racial conflicts and national frontiers. ... clearly manifests to all that note of the Catholic Church which rejects discord, flees division, and abhors all disputes which agitate nations and sometimes bring them to utter ruin.[51]

---

51 Pius XII, Encyclical on the Promotion of Catholic Missions, *Evangelii Praecones* (2 June 1951) § 2,3, at The Holy See, https://www.vatican.va/content/pius-xii/en/encyclicals/documents/hf_p-xii_enc_02061951_evangelii-praecones.html.

CHAPTER III

Analysis of *Things Fall Apart*

A Critical Interpretation of Achebe's Point of View

Achebe's aim was essentially a reconstruction of history. He saw the need to recreate and represent his tradition which had, for so long, been presented by white writers who knew little or nothing about Igbo tradition and culture. As a real Igbo man, he wanted to give a voice not only to the Igbo culture but also to the African heritage. It is for this reason that he writes 'English' in Igbo across his works. As a proud Igbo man, he made it his duty and responsibility to project his way of life to the world, especially to those who, unknown to themselves, are ignorant of it. People like the District Commissioner in *Things Fall Apart* who made irrational conclusions about the culture. As illustrated in his critical essay on Joseph Conrad's *Heart of Darkness*, Achebe was keen on presenting the real image of Africa, which he thought had been somewhat written off by white writers.

As Alison Searle puts it in *The Role of Missions in 'Things Fall Apart' and Nervous Conditions,* "Achebe deliberately attempts to construct a variegated, unsentimental and empathetic image of Igbo life prior to their personal contact with English culture and imperialism." Achebe wanted his novel to teach his readers, especially Igbo people that,

Their past was not one long night of savagery from which the first Europeans acting on God's behalf delivered them. He wanted to point out the values of the two distinctive cultures by appreciating the diverse nature of the colonial encounter, which carelessly destroyed and imposed its culture on the other, but also opened opportunities and provided certain benefits. In *Things Fall Apart*, Achebe demonstrates the ways in which the Igbo people chose to participate in the changing order of things. He made it clear that rigid opposition was not celebrated among the Igbos.[52]

Hence, she presented the Igbo flexibility and response to change to a new order.

Despite the resistance offered by Okonkwo, *Things Fall Apart* presents scenes of no opposition to the white culture. They, however, welcomed the new order in their land by offering them lands for their establishment. Therefore, Achebe presents the peaceful nature of the Igbo tradition, which is open to change and welcoming to other cultures. The Igbo man was in his rightful place, and the white man (the colonial regime) intruded on his peace, or better still, invaded another man's land and imposed his way of life on the rightful owner of the land. The Igbo man did not lord it over the intruder, and this shows how civilized the Igbo society was right from the beginning. The supposed and presumed civilized western culture, on the contrary, seemed to be the uncivilized one and was reluctant to acknowledge it. *Things Fall Apart* is an ironic attempt to write back to the dominant imperial historians a riposte to the District Commissioner's intention to write a "reasonable paragraph" on the incident of Okonkwo's demise.

As Achebe puts it in *The Role of the Writer in a New Nation*, "Historians everywhere are re-writing the stories of the new nations — replacing short, garbled, despised history with a more sympathetic

52 Alison Searle, "The Role of Missions in *Things Fall Apart* and Nervous Conditions." *Literature & Theology*, Vol. 21, No. 1 (March 2007): 50, https://www.jstor.org/stable/23927309.

account." According to him, it is natural and necessary because these said writers must begin to correct the prejudices that generations of detractors created about the Negro. He cited, for instance, Thomas Jefferson, who believed that the black race had a lower grade of talent than the whites.

The astonishing thing, as he puts it, was that these prejudices were not only expressed by the unenlightened but were also supported by men of distinction. Hence, as one of the writers of a new nation, Achebe's point of view is made clear with *Things Fall Apart*, which wrests the rights to Igbo history from the imperialists who termed the culture 'primitive.'[53]

Achebe's philosophy was consistent in his critique of Joseph Conrad's *Heart of Darkness*. In *An Image of Africa: Racism in Conrad's Heart of Darkness*, he presented a white fellow's point of view about negroes thus:

> An older man going the same way as I turned and remarked to me how very young they came these days. I agreed. Then he asked me if I was a student too. I said no, I was a teacher. What did I teach? African literature. Now that was funny, he said, because he knew a fellow who taught the same thing, or perhaps it was African history, in a certain Community College not far from here. It always surprised him, he went on to say, because he never had thought of Africa as having that kind of stuff, you know. By this time, I was walking much faster. "Oh well," I heard him say finally, behind me, 'I guess I have to take your course to find out.'[54]

Achebe's emphasis on "he asked if I was a student too" explains much about the West's view of the black man as the white man's burden,

---

53 Chinua Achebe, G.D. Killam, "The role of a writer in a new nation," *African writers on African writing,* (1973), 7–8.

54 Achebe, "An Image of Africa" in *Heart of Darkness*, Ed. Paul B. Armstrong, (London: W. W. Norton and Co., 2017) 307.

just as Rudyard Kipling would put it. The thought that Achebe was a teacher destabilized the fellow who wanted to take Achebe's course to find out what exactly it was he taught. Hence, Achebe made it his duty to rectify such irrational beliefs held by the white man and assert that Africa has a history, and of course, its own literature.

Furthermore, he believes that "the African people did not learn about culture from Europeans; that their societies were not mindless but had a philosophy with great depth, value, and beauty; that they had poetry and, above all, they had dignity. It was this dignity that many Africans all but lost during the colonial period and it is this that they must now regain."[55] He noted that, "the worst thing that can happen to any people is the loss of their dignity and self-respect." In his famous novel, he demonstrated that the writer's duty is to help the people regain their dignity and self-respect by showing them in human terms that which they had lost about their culture and what happened to them in the past. To perform this task well, he needed to have proper knowledge and sense of history.

In addition, a writer is meant to put things in order, correct and make right the wrongs the people had been made to believe over time about their own culture. He must know that "the past needs to be recreated not only for the enlightenment of our detractors but even more for our own education, because we must know that the past with all its imperfections never lacked dignity."[56] One crucial thing for Achebe is that cultures have their good and bad points and, therefore, in recreating the history of the Igbo culture, he tried to eulogize its good points and, at the same time, did not pretend over the bad parts.

In other words, he was able to find and accurately identify the two sides of the culture, that is, the good and the bad sides. We see him criticize, through his characters, some of the cultural beliefs he considered despicable, like the killing of twins, the enigma of the

---

55 Achebe, Killam, "The role of a writer in a new nation," 8.
56 Achebe, Killam, "The role of a writer in a new nation," 9.

evil forest, the o*su* caste system et al. As he put it, "the writer's integrity is determined by his or her capacity to overcome the temptation
of selecting only those facts which fascinate him. He must also pin-
point the other things that do not flatter him in the real sense. By so
doing, he will be branding himself as a trustworthy witness and will
render credibility and integrity to his person and to the world that
he is trying to re-create".

Achebe factored in these principles in his works and it is only
for this reason that he has been termed the great inventor of African
literature and culture. He admitted that Igbo history, like those of
other tribes, was not only an idyllic experience but had its off-put-
ting sides as well.

Considering the peculiar nature of the Igbo culture, Achebe
thought it would be useless to take off from the present without
trying to repair the foundations first. This he made clear in *The Role
of a Writer in a New Nation,* thus: "We must first set the scene which
is authentically African, then what follows will be meaningful and
deep." In other words, the fastest way to understand the future is
the past. There ought to be no confusion of values among writers
of new nations, and therefore, they are to be concerned mostly with
the question of human values while avoiding any shoddiness in their
work. He took it as his responsibility and collaborated in the building of a new nation and the reconstruction of the origins of his own
culture. In this light, he did not only enrich himself but has enriched
the whole world with the culture he recuperated.

Similarly, in *An Image of Africa,* Achebe point out other aspects
that can serve as a barometer for understanding him and his intent
as an African writer. He is not just an Igbo man but also a proud
and happy African whose aim was to promote the great values of
his culture and to make it known to the world that African history and literature exist. Overall, he is Keen to wipe out ignorance,
not only from the least educated but also and especially from most
western scholars who have termed Africa the heart of darkness and

a burden to the white man. Considering the description of Conrad in *Heart of Darkness*, Africa, for a long time, has been regarded as a mere "glimpse of rush walls, of peaked grass-roofs, a burst of yells, a whirl of black limbs, a mass of hands clapping, of feet stamping, of bodies swaying, of eyes rolling under the droop of heavy and motionless foliage. The atmosphere a black and incomprehensible frenzy, everything was silent."[57]

The repetition of 'black,' 'frenzy,' and 'silence' by Conrad is appalling and builds up to the description of Africa as prehistoric. Again, there were no attributes of humanity lent to the natives; Conrad saw them as very different from himself, especially by the way he described the human body in some detail. His narrator saw no unified human body or group of people. Rather, he saw a whirl of black limbs, a mass of hands, feet, bodies, and eyes, all engaged in different actions. He deliberately did not assign a whole body to them for a purpose; else, it could have been easier to use a 'group of people in actions' rather than using the different parts of the body and giving the impression that what he saw was not humans, but things appearing like humans. By doing so, he denied humanity not solely to the Congo natives but also the African continent as a whole.

Achebe was critical of Conrad's choice of words and language in *Heart of Darkness*. Although Conrad recognized himself in this prehistoric man, the fear of being termed prehistoric and therefore sharing ancestry with the Negro haunted him. He was too uncomfortable to accept the reality of his prehistoric origin, which would have tied him more closely with the Negroes he met on his journey. His description continues: "We were cut off from the comprehension of our surroundings; we glided past like phantoms, wondering and secretly appalled, as sane men would be before an enthusiastic outbreak in a madhouse."[58] Conrad alluded to Africa and Africans as

---

57 Paul B. Armstrong, ed., *Heart of Darkness*, (London: W. W. Norton and Co., 2017), 35.
58 Armstrong, *Heart of Darkness*, 36.

being "an enthusiastic outbreak in a madhouse", which is very different from what it really was in the eyes of the natives themselves. The white man was a stranger in Africa and, therefore, knew nothing but his own culture and tradition. He was unable to identify that a new and different culture was in existence in the new surroundings he found himself. Perhaps he expected to meet the same conditions of his home after traveling more than halfway across the world. Clearly, he prided his own culture as being superior to others; yet he had no real knowledge of others. He went as far as seeking to impose his culture on others, as we see in the case of the imperial regime in Igboland in *Things Fall Apart*.

The white man pretended not to understand his kinship with Africa: "We could not understand because we were too far and could not remember, because we were traveling in the night of first ages, of those ages that are gone, leaving hardly a sign — and no memories"[59] In Conrad's representation, being "too far" could be an allusion to the supremacy of the western culture over other cultures. Whereas in *Things Fall Apart,* it was the western culture that proved to be uncivilized, having no respect for natives and imposing itself on the Igbo culture. Rather than seeking a platform for coexistence — the hallmark of true civilization — the white man was determined to suppress all that did not belong to him.

Hence, Achebe set out to correct the Western world's erroneous perceptions, ideas, and beliefs about Africa. He wanted to change the prejudices of people who had never been to Africa and change the negative perceptions and emotions people had about his continent. He wanted to correct the misleading representations of an African image created by some Western scholars. He proved that there is a lot more to what was told and probably believed, about Africa. (Bekler, 97) We see this in the traditional Igbo setting of Umuofia, that the Igbo people, before the arrival of the white man, had

---

59 Ibid.

an established culture and tradition with a welcoming democratic disposition. We also see that, even though they were thought to be primitive, African tribes lived their own lives and had traditions and cultures that were unique to them, and were already civilized in their own nature with functional systems of government.

In a recent interview with Pete Edochie, he sheds more light on Achebe's attempt to represent the invasion of the culture of the people and the resistance offered by the people. According to Edochie, "that is what *Things Fall Apart* is all about. Achebe successfully portrayed what the Igbo man represents when it comes to defending his culture." Things fell apart in the Igbo society when the white man entered with the European culture and shattered an effective society. As Mahanta Pona and Maut Dibakar put it in their concluding notes in the *Impact of the colonizer on the colonized,* Achebe did not only attack the colonizers for their thoughtless destruction of the so-called primitive culture and religion, but he also criticizes the drawbacks of the Igbo society. In the novel, the colonizers used their religion as a tool to achieve their aim. Achebe portrays their employment of barbaric force to pacify the natives. He made it clear "that the Igbo culture and religion in spite of their drawbacks and superstitions, proved to be wiser in much of its direct clashes with the Christian faith."[60]

Achebe is said to have invented African literature and history. It is not that there was never anything written about Africa before his emergence, but because, as a historian, he was able to "use literature as a social document where he preserves and records his society's traditions and experiences."[61] He compiled a comprehensive account of an African culture that sheds new light on earlier writings by other African authors. Thus, he established African literature

---

60 Mahanta Pona, Maut Dibakar. "The Impact of Colonizer on the Colonized: A Postcolonial Study of Nigerian Igbo Culture and History in Chinua Achebe's *Things Fall Apart*." *IOSR Journal of Humanities and Social Science*, Vol. 19, no.11 (Nov.2014), 8.

61 Ibid, 8.

by reconstructing a history that had been misunderstood and poorly represented for some time.

As observed by Bekler, Achebe demonstrated his ability as a hermeneutist in *Things Fall Apart* by using Igbo words and translating them into English meanings. He was able to achieve his objective of communicating his beliefs, ideas, and observations to the rest of the world by carefully selecting his language. He wrote in English because he thought it would be effective than the Igbo language in conveying the true face of Africa to the world. He regards himself as a teacher whose primary responsibility is to cultivate a positive alternative perspective on Africa that is distinct from the one that his Eurocentric counterparts have previously projected.[62]

According to Korang, Kwaku Larbi in *Making a Post-Eurocentric Humanity: Tragedy, Realism, and Things Fall Apart*, "Achebe is an African writer writing back to his eurocentric predecessors and contemporaries, in protest against their aesthetic, humanistic and ethical bad faith where their representations of Africa is concerned."[63] In other words, with *Things Fall Apart*, he practically nullifies the models of his Eurocentric predecessors that conferred humanistic discretion and knowledge exclusively on the west.

He mostly criticized Conrad for aesthetically portraying Africa in an obscure and hazy space with no continental humanity, and for having denied humanity to Africa at the level of language. Conrad indirectly induced in his European readers the feeling of horror as he floods them with imagery of a horrifying African darkness that threatens to contaminate and submerge the European light in the imperial encounter between the two continents. For him, Africa is void of humanity and civilization and, therefore, a contradiction of Europe.[64] In response to this, Achebe made a realistic and humanistic

---

62 Bekler, "The true face of pre-colonial Africa in *Things Fall Apart*," 97.
63 Kwaku Larbi Korang, "Making a Post-Eurocentric Humanity: Tragedy, Realism, and *Things Fall Apart*," *Research in African Literatures*, Vol. 42, No. 2 (Summer 2011), 2.
64 Ibid, 4.

representation of the clan of Umuofia (Igbo) as a world full of sense and order in relation to the western world. He aimed to represent Africa as the dream state, as the sensible and real world. Knowing fully well that the challenge for the African writer in opposition to his European counterparts is to restore humanity to Africa, the novel *Things Fall Apart* was conceived to recuperate the lost and tarnished African aesthetics for the reclamation of African humanity. Hence, the expectation is to make the readers agree that humanity exceeds the geographical bounds of Europe.

Achebe and the Igbo Culture

Achebe was a proud Igbo man. In *Things Fall Apart*, he demonstrated his love for his culture and tradition by illustrating the daily life of the Igbo community. In doing so, he restored the common cultural sense of his people's past. His detailed portrayal of Umuofia and its environments illustrated how much he valued his own culture and how important he saw every Igbo tradition to be. This is seen in his translation of one of the culturally unique languages of Africa (Igbo), its proverbs and folklore, into the language of the colonizers, thereby showing his love for his own culture and language, and his intent to give a voice to it. He did this to facilitate easy and worldwide comprehension of his own culture. Through his realistic imagery and the representation of a visible humanity in Umuofia, he leads the reader by hand into the reality of the Igbo community, thereby making the reader feel a part of the entire experience. Right from the beginning of the novel, Achebe carefully takes the reader through the social and cultural peculiarities that Umuofia has developed over time as unique responses and adaptations to the existential challenges of survival. He wants the reader to understand that Umuofia's unique characteristics serve a humanizing purpose.[65]

---

65 Korang, "Making a Post-Eurocentric Humanity," 16.

Achebe illustrated with delight the cultural heritage of his origin, a project that could only be carried out after a long range of studies in a particular field.

According to an Igbo adage, *an adult does not stay in the house and watch a she-goat suffer the pains of parturition in its tether.* Achebe did not fancy the idea of staying aloof and watching his cherished cultural heritage altered in any way by people who knew little or nothing about it. Hence, he made it his duty to present a fairer, more accurate picture. As he often said, the writers of the new nations must teach and enlighten people about their culture. He stressed that "Africa did not hear of culture for the first time from Europe, but had a philosophy of great depth and value and poetry and above all, dignity." Therefore, it is this dignity they lost to colonialism that needed to be restored. Achebe intended to maintain and reproduce the actual world he inherited from his ancestors. We see him participate fully in his culture in some scenes of *Things Fall Apart*. He not only represented life in Umuofia but, in telling the story of the clan, he made himself a part of it. In this way, he inscribed into a lasting documentation that which he did not want to be lost, that is, his tradition. Very importantly, his tale is credible because he was an integral part of it. We could see him take a stand in the unfolding events of his novel. Some instances of this include his description of the customs of Umuofia, his convictions about life as manifested through his characters, his thorough description of *ogbanje* children and how they could be liberated (especially in the case of Ezimma), his clear description of a traditional herbal cure for malaria, his belief in a man's chances of rising to greatness by dint of hard work and through the wealth he eventually acquires, and his respect for the elders as mouthpieces of the oracle. His expert piecing of these aspects of his novel reveals much about the writer — him.

Nor did Achebe hesitate to reveal the dark sides of the Igbo tradition. As presented elsewhere in this work, he renounced, through the words of some of his characters, some traditions like the killing of twin babies and the enigma of the evil forest. In the scene where Ikemefuna was killed, we hear Ezeudu (one of the oldest men in Umuofia) condemn Okonkwo's evil act thus: "That boy calls you father. Do not bear a hand in his death." Again, through Obierika, in one of his conversations with Okonkwo over the killing of the young boy, he said:

> I cannot understand why you refused to come with us to kill that boy," he asked Obierika. "Because I did not want to," Obierika replied sharply. "I had something better to do." "You sound as if you question the authority and the decision of the Oracle, who said he should die." "I do not. Why should I? But the Oracle did not ask me to carry out its decision." "But someone had to do it. If we were all afraid of blood, it would not be done. And what do you think the Oracle would do then?
>
> You know very well, Okonkwo, that I am not afraid of blood and if anyone tells you that I am, he is telling a lie. And let me tell you one thing, my friend. If I were you I would have stayed at home. What you have done will not please the Earth. It is the kind of action for which the goddess wipes out whole families."[...] "But if the Oracle said that my son should be killed I would neither dispute it nor be the one to do it.[66]

Achebe nudges the reader to decide for himself who was right and who was wrong. He challenges the psychology of the human person to reason out particular situations within the contexts of the era. He told a full story by not only providing idyllic scenarios that would glorify his Igbo culture and tradition. He was able to present the good as well as the bad, just the way he saw them, all the while conveying his constant moral combat with the issues presented. Speaking through Ezeudu in a conversation with another clansman,

---

66 Achebe, *Things Fall Apart,* 48.

he condemned the tradition of casting into the *evil forest* all who died during the week of peace. "They have that custom in Obodoani. If a man dies at this time, he is not buried but cast into the Evil Forest. It is a bad custom, which these people observe because they lack understanding. They throw away large numbers of men and women without burial. And what is the result? Their clan is full of the evil spirits of these unburied dead, hungry to do harm to the living."(*Things Fall Apart*) Seemingly, Achebe intended to restore sanity and hope where it was lacking in the customs and traditions of Umuofia and, by extension, the Igbo tribe.

True to his Igbo origin, it is significant how Achebe used Igbo market days. There are typically four market days in a week according to the traditional Igbo calendar: *eke, orie, afor* and *nkwo*. Every community in Igboland has a market named after one of the four aforementioned market days, such as Eke market or Afor market. The days are based on the four cardinal points: Afo corresponds to the north, Nkwo to the south, Eke to the east, and Orie to the west. The four days are decked with business and other cultural and religious significance, and their purpose was to create a social structure throughout Igboland.

The Igbos did not make plans without taking their four market days into consideration. *Eke, Orie, Nkwo,* and *Afor,* were very important to the tribe. Meetings and appointments were scheduled based on market days. The market days also influenced the adoption of traditional Igbo surnames like Nwokeke, Nwokorie, Nwokenkwo and Nwokafor, where "Nwoke" stands for "man". People were named according to the market day of their birth. In today's Igbo society, such names still exist, having been passed from generation to generation. However, with members of contemporary Igbo society now adopting their names directly from their immediate parents, market-day names could become extinct sooner than later.

Those who have busied themselves with dissecting Achebe's works have not given attention to his frequent use of 'time and numbers'. In

Things Fall Apart, he frequently used the numbers "three" and "seven". In the Igbo tradition, numbers 'three' and 'seven' encode perfection and completion, respectively. They are often used in oral tradition: 'three market days'; 'seven days and seven nights'; 'three wives'; 'seven years'; 'three converts'; 'three days later'; etc., they all allude to symbolic perfection and completion of events in particular occasions. For instance, most crucial in *Things Fall Apart* was the importance of the number of human heads Okonkwo brought home from wars he fought. His destiny was, in a way, connected to the number of heads he claimed in war. In the second chapter, we read that "in Umuofia's latest war he was the first to bring home a human head. That was his fifth head and he was not an old man yet." The number of heads was significant because it could have also had a connection to his tragic death.

Considering the significance of numbers in *Things Fall Apart*, and in Igbo culture as a whole, Okonkwo's achievement of five heads was two heads shy of completion. To arrive at this, it was necessary that, by fate or chance, two other heads be sacrificed as a mark of perfection prefiguring the climax of the story. Ikemefuna proved to be the sixth head, and then, in this ominous turn of events, points to Okonkwo's imminent suicide. In other words, Ikemefuna's could be counted as the sixth head Okonkwo was able to claim to prove his bravery and gallantry. Okonkwo did not need to partake in the killing of the lad, he was even advised by his friend not to go, but he was wary of being thought weak. "Dazed with fear, Okonkwo drew his matchet and cut him down." It was his sixth head, even if he did not bring it home. For the story to reach its completion and climax, Okonkwo's head became the seventh. Like the heads count, there were other hidden meanings behind numbers in the events occurring in Umuofia — Igboland. Therefore, numbers (especially 'three' and 'seven') were significant in determining the fate of individuals in precolonial Igbo society.

Achebe presented two contrasting but noble viewpoints on Igbo nature in *Things Fall Apart*. There was Okonkwo, a symbol of resistance to the imposing western culture, and a man of high moral standing and of honor among his people. And then there were Obierika, Ezeudu, Akunna and his maternal uncle Uchendu, who were more logical. Though they too were great and fearless warriors who were accorded enormous respect in the clan, they were rather calm and more rational than Okonkwo. Through these characters, Achebe called some Igbo traditions to question. Obierika was hesitant about the oracle's verdict for Ikemefuna to be killed. Okonkwo would say to him later, "You sound as if you question the authority and the decision of the Oracle, who said he should die." While Obierika could not overturn the oracle's decision, he did say to Okonkwo, "If I were you I would have stayed at home." It is safe to say that Obierika disliked Okonkwo's excesses but, knowing his friend, he only declared what he would do if in the same position, perhaps knowing Okonkwo as one who was too obstinate to take advice. More of Obierika's easy-going disposition is seen in chapter eight where he disagreed with some of the clan's traditions.

In a conversation with Okonkwo, about the law of the land which forbade men with the *ozo* title from tapping their tall palm trees, he said: "Sometimes I wish I had not taken the *ozo* title. It wounds my heart to see these young men killing palm trees in the name of tapping." "It is so indeed," agreed Okonkwo. "But the law of the land must be obeyed." "I don't know how we got that law," said Obierika. "In many other clans a man of title is not forbidden to climb the palm tree. Here we say he cannot climb the tall tree but he can tap the short ones standing on the ground. It is like Dimaragana, who would not lend his knife for cutting up dog-meat because the dog was taboo to him, but offered to use his teeth." Obierika was a symbol of light and change in the clan who approached inherited tradition with a good measure of rationality. He regretted having taken the *ozo* title, because he wondered why a so-called achievement would limit a man from engaging in everyday activities — like tapping his palm trees.

Ezeudu, like Obierika, was dismayed by the excesses of tradition. Concerning the tradition of throwing people who died during the week of peace into the evil forest, he said, "It is a bad custom which these people observe because they lack understanding". He also warned Okonkwo against participating in the killing of Ikemefuna: "That boy calls you father. Do not bear a hand in his death." He continued without entertaining Okonkwo's defense: "Yes, Umuofia has decided to kill him. The Oracle of the Hills and the Caves has pronounced it. They will take him outside Umuofia as is the custom, and kill him there. But I want you to have nothing to do with it. He calls you his father." Exhibiting sympathy and affection in the face of draconian traditions, Ezeudu suggests that the Igbo culture has sources of censure and self-purification within itself. He was not alone. Okonkwo's maternal uncle, Uchendu, was described as a calm, wise man who picked his words with great care. He welcomed Okonkwo like his own son during his exile in Mbanta and showed his wisdom at their family gathering when he addressed Okonkwo:

> These are now your kinsmen." He waved at his sons and daughters. "You think you are the greatest sufferer in the world? Do you know that men are sometimes banished for life? Do you know that men sometimes lose all their yams and even their children? I had six wives once. I have none now except that young girl who knows not her right from her left. Do you know how many children I have buried — children I begot in my youth and strength? Twenty-two. I did not hang myself, and I am still alive. If you think you are the greatest sufferer in the world ask my daughter, Akueni, how many twins she has borne and thrown away.[67]

Uchendu played a significant role in Achebe's representation of the Igbo culture. Through him, Achebe portrayed the paternal affection which western writers seemed to neglect, and the benevolence and tenderness that Okonkwo was too ashamed to express.

---

67 Achebe, *Things Fall Apart*, 95.

The colonialists neither observed these character traits nor were they captured by western scholars. Had they observed it, they would not have failed to recognize the civility emanating from homesteads, which would have been a pointer to a civilizing tribe. Umuofia had men of wisdom, persuasive orators (as proven by their use of proverbs and eloquence in speech), and men of high social standing who could have provided the watershed moments the Igbo culture needed for positive transformation. It was this promise, of a tribe which, even though steep in primitivity and barbarism at the time, was going to find its way to the future, that Achebe sought to project to the world. He wrote it in the language of the empire so that many could understand, yet not leaving out his language. As a post-colonial writer, he was keen to build a new nation, to restore dignity to a tribe which had been denied access to excellence in several ways. He sought to give back humanity to a tribe which had suffered brash impositions from the colonial administration. He projected the parts of the Igbo people (Africa) which the British failed to see in their quest to conquer and enslave natives in their own land.

Things Fall Apart ultimately showed the Igbos' ability to adapt to a new order. In an ever-changing world, every culture would, at some point, encounter other cultures and be influenced to change and adapt. Malinowski, an English anthropologist, in his theory of cultural functionalism, did say that no culture remains 'primitive' forever, as they are bound to evolve over time and adapt themselves to global sociocultural set patterns. The Igbo culture did change after its encounter with the English culture. The Umuofia at the beginning of *Things Fall Apart* differed from the one at the end. The advent of Christianity changed Umuofia; but with Okonkwo's tragic end, Achebe further demonstrates that some form of loss often precedes change. As Korang surmised in *Making a Post-Eurocentric Humanity*, "for Okonkwo to recover himself he must vitally lose some of himself, and, his situation is emblematic of Umuofia at large. For Umuofia to find its normative corporate Self, it must vitally lose some of itself." Okonkwo, who unreflectively configured his personality and public actions to align with Umuofia's pre-set cultural patterns, embodied the clan's cultural limitations and irrationality. Through Ezeudu, Achebe conveyed the certainty of change when, in a conversation with two men of the clan, he noted that the punishment for breaking the sacred week of peace had become mild compared to what it used to be. "It has not always been so," he said. "My father told me that he had been told that in the past a man who broke the peace was dragged on the ground through the village until he died. But after a while this custom was stopped because it spoiled the peace which it was meant to preserve."

Achebe portrayed an Igbo society that was open to change. The coming of change may have been long, but it was sure to come. Ezeudu's statement proved that Umuofia was already changing, even before the arrival of the colonialists.

Achebe's Narrative Style

With its literary and complex form, *Things Fall Apart* uses an omniscient narrator to create an intersection between narrative construction and colonial and historical recuperation by documenting the meeting of two worlds. Achebe combines tragic, ironic, and comic modes in his narration, representing many diverse voices of the same culture. He enriched this work — as other works of his — with folklore, myths, proverbs, and rhetorical devices such as personification and onomatopoeia. His narration evokes a vast and complex world that does not limit itself to the closed walls of the British and Igbo cultures but also interrogates the enigma of colonialism in its entirety.

In *Things Fall Apart*, Achebe illustrates the divergent cultural narratives of the west and the Igbo by mixing the Igbo traditional oral mode with the European literary discourse. As sustained by Dannenberg, "if a postcolonial author chooses to write in the language of the colonizer, he or she must use original strategies to give the narrative a truly postcolonial spirit. Hence, Achebe proved his ability to endow his narrative with a truly postcolonial complexity."[68] This is seen in Achebe's complex narrative effort in giving voices to the different characters in this work and projecting "the complexities both of Igbo culture and of the meeting of cultures."[69] (Dannenberg). He was able to insert the nuances of the Igbo traditional culture into the western literary form. For instance, the frequent recurrence of repetitive phrases and words, storytelling, and traditional chants; the frequent use of Igbo proverbs, and the insertion of tribal customs in *Things Fall Apart* all allude to the nature of Igbo oral language and custom. In other words, Achebe successfully integrates the literary narrative elements of both cultures in his work. As Jarica Linn Watts wrote in *He does not understand our customs:*

> Achebe composes his work in the language of the colonizer, but integrates folklore, proverbs, tribal customs, and the performance of oral storytelling in order to evoke Igbo tradition and to force the reader to acknowledge the story he tells on his own terms. [...] by infusing with traditional Igbo words and phrases (*obi, egwugwu, iyi-uwa*, etc.), Achebe's work, reshapes and re-contextualizes the language of the colonizer — and the implicit power structures within it — in a specifically hybridized form of English.[70]

In the first chapter of this book, the importance of oral tradition in the Igbo culture was surveyed; we saw that the Igbo people never had any documented work to preserve their history, and that their story was passed orally from one generation to the next. Therefore, following the repetitive structures in the narrator's and several

---

68 Dannenberg, Hilary, "The many voices of *Things Fall Apart,*" *Interventions,* Vol. 11, no.2 (2009): 176.
69 Ibid.
70 Linn Watts Jarica, "He does not understand our customs", *Journal of Postcolonial Writing.* Vol. 46, no. 1, (February 2010): 65.

characters' expressions and words (often used sequentially to describe the same event or scene), and the recurrence of storytelling, Achebe, in his work, shows the importance of the oral tradition in Igbo culture and the ability of the Igbo language to preserve its culture.

He did this by including in his narration, storytelling, through which important and core information about the culture is passed. For instance, we see the characters tell stories they have been told in their childhood, and of which they, in return, retell to their children on different occasions in the novel. Okonkwo's wives and children take turns for storytelling. An example is the scene where Ekwefi told the story about the birds and the cunning and ungrateful Tortoise, of how the Tortoise was able to deceive the birds and have them lend him their feathers for him to attend a feast in the sky with them for his own gain, and which later led to his destruction. There are different stories of such, like that of Cat and Tortoise wrestling against Yams. These stories were used to convey and preserve some important moral aspects of the culture. Again, Achebe employed some Igbo words in the novel, not that he did not know their meaning or equivalents in English, but he purposely used them in the language and culture he intended to preserve.

Most notably, following Jonathan Greenberg's assertion in *Okonkwo and the Storyteller*, that "Achebe's novel can be seen as a portrait of Igbo culture precisely at the moment of transition from story to novel,"[71] that is, from oral to written form, one might agree with Linn Watts that the repetitive phrases simply "highlight the difference between the spoken and the printed sphere, the African oral rather than the English 'literary' tradition."

Regarding Achebe's distinctive modes of representation in *Things Fall Apart,* this work has already identified the frequent 'repetition'. Repetitive structures in quick successions and in form of meta-narratives is another. The opening paragraph began with the

---

71 Jonathan Greenberg, "Okonkwo and the Storyteller: Death, Accident, and Meaning in Achebe and Benjamin," (2007): 2.

narrator's description of Okonkwo's prowess and possible affiliation to the clan's progenitor and, hence, his influence on the entire clan. On display was a simple and smooth flow of orality in narration, hence, the exportation of the oral method of telling folktales as the novel begins with the account of Okonkwo's wrestling bout with Amalinze years prior.

The first two parts of the novel present series of quick repetitions, sometimes in the same paragraphs and at other times in different chapters. For instance, in chapter three, the narrator started by saying that "Okonkwo did not have the start in life which many young men usually had. He did not inherit a barn from his father. There was no barn to inherit." This was repeated in the eighth paragraph of the same chapter: "Okonkwo did not have the start in life which many young men had. He neither inherited a barn nor a title." Similarly, Okonkwo continued his sequential interior meditation on Ezinma by saying that "she should have been a boy"; and this he repeated several times across the novel whenever he thought about her. Other examples are the frequent recurrences of "Okonkwo was not a man of thought but of action"; "Ezinma unlike most children, called her mother by her name"; "for three years Ikemefuna lived in Okonkwo's household" and several other similar cases of repetition.

Most notable, perhaps, is Ogbuefi Ezeugo's consecutive actions in bellowing at the clan's gathering in the second chapter: "At last Ogbuefi Ezeugo stood up in the midst of them and bellowed four times, "*Umuofia kwenu*," and on each occasion, he faced a different direction and seemed to push the air with a clenched fist. And ten thousand men answered, "Yaa!" Another was Egwugwu's successive remarks during the settlement of a dispute between Uzowulu and his in-laws. The *Evil Forest* started by bellowing the gathering three good times with "*Umuofia Kwenu*" and successive "Uzowulu's body I salute you" and "Odukwe's body I salute you" which were repeated on different occasions. These repetitions portray the Igbos' habitual way of life, that of storytelling, and Achebe transitions it from oral to written form.

Furthermore, Achebe's use of Igbo proverbs added more spice to his narration. In the first chapter, he said "among the Igbo the art of conversation is regarded very highly, and proverbs are the palm oil with which words are eaten." This is clear in most of his works. With it, he showed his place in the Igbo culture, as half of a real Igbo man's discourse is laced with proverbs. Achebe shows how the Igbos draw wisdom from or infuse it into their proverbs. Some scholars think that proverbs are key to understanding Achebe's novels because he uses them to emphasize the values of the society he is portraying.

Achebe also used other important narrative aspects like flashbacks or back looping and descriptive modes to enhance the narration. We see a lot of memory work whereby characters recall what happened in the clan in the past. His back-and-forth looping greatly enriched his work. Among other examples from *Things Fall Apart,* it would be interesting to consider the beginning of the first chapter, where the narrator recalled what had happened twenty years ago when Okonkwo was eighteen and in the fourteenth chapter during Okonkwo's exile. Here is the flashback:

> Okonkwo was well known throughout the nine villages and even beyond. His fame rested on solid personal achievements. As a young man of eighteen he had brought honour to his village by throwing Amalinze the Cat. Amalinze was the great wrestler who for seven years was unbeaten, from Umuofia to Mbaino. He was called the Cat because his back would never touch the earth. It was this man that Okonkwo threw in a fight which the old men agreed was one of the fiercest since the founder of their town engaged a spirit of the wild for seven days and seven nights. [...] That was many years ago, twenty years or more. ...Unoka, for that was his father's name, had died ten years ago. In his days he was lazy and improvident and

was quite incapable of thinking about tomorrow. [....] His name
was Uchendu, and it was he who had received Okonkwo's mother
twenty and ten years before when she had been brought home
from Umuofia to be buried with her people. Okonkwo was only a
boy then and Uchendu still remembered him crying the traditional
farewell: "Mother, mother, mother is going." That was many years
ago.[72]

Similarly, Obierika, Ezeudu, Uchendu, etc., recalled events of
old in the history of the clan. An example, upon the news of Ndu-
lue's death in the eighth chapter, Obierika recalled his youthful days:
"I remember when I was a young boy there was a song about them.
He could not do anything without telling her."

Under further analysis, we see Achebe give life to everything
about Umuofia by animating even the least inanimate things in the
clan. His descriptive strategies are clearly seen in how he described
every aspect of the clan's events and activities, its surroundings,
and the natural world. For events like clan gatherings, feasts, celebrations, customs, etc., he gave complete and accurate accounts of
everything they did and how they did them. An example is the scene
in the fourteenth chapter where the youngest of Uchendu's sons,
Amikwu, was taking a wife:

They sat in a big circle on the ground and the young bride in the
center with a hen in her right hand. Uchendu before her, holding
the ancestral staff of the family. The men stood outside the circle,
watching. Their wives also. It was evening and the sun was setting,
Uchendu's eldest daughter, Njide, asked her" "Remember that if
you do not answer truthfully you will suffer or even die at child-
birth," she began.[73]

---

72 Achebe, *Things Fall Apart*, 1, 91.
73 Achebe, *Things Fall Apart*, 93.

For a literary end, the narrator described even little scenarios and things that would not have been missed were they left out. Again, in chapter fourteen, we see a thorough description of natural elements in context:

At last the rain came. It was sudden and tremendous. For two or three moons the sun had been gathering strength till it seemed to breathe a breath of fire on the earth. All the grass had long been scorched brown, and the sands felt like live coals to the feet. Evergreen trees wore a dusty coat of brown. The birds were silenced in the forests, and the world lay panting under the live, vibrating heat. And then came the clap of thunder. It was an angry, metallic and thirsty clap, unlike the deep and liquid rumbling of the rainy season. A mighty wind arose and filled the air with dust. Palm trees swayed as the wind combed their leaves into flying crests like strange and fantastic coiffure. When the rain finally came, it was in large, solid drops of frozen water which the people called "the nuts of the water of heaven." They were hard and painful on the body as they fell, yet young people ran about happily picking up the cold nuts and throwing them into their mouths to melt. The earth quickly came to life and the birds in the forests fluttered around and chirped merrily. A vague scent of life and green vegetation was diffused in the air. As the rain began to fall more soberly and in smaller liquid drops, children sought for shelter, and all were happy, refreshed and thankful.[74]

In addition, amidst many instances in *Things Fall Apart*, examples of his use of rhetorical devices like personifications and onomatopoeia abound. For instance, in chapter thirteen, where he reproduced and personified the hollowed-out instrument, *ekwe*, "Go-di-di-go-go-di-go. Di-go-go-digo. It was the *ekwe* talking to the clan. ...Dum!

---

74 Achebe, *Things Fall Apart*, 91.

Dum! Dum! boomed the cannon at intervals. ...the *ekwe* began to talk, and the cannon shattered the silence", and also, in the second chapter, "*Gome, gome, gome, gome,* boomed the hollow metal."

Here, he made the instruments talk by saying that the "*ekwe* began to talk", and silence was animated in "the cannon 'shattered' the silence." Instances such as these are abundant in the novel as Achebe carefully selected his devices to suit his narrative strategy.

Achebe's critics have notably failed to consider his emblematic excessive use of nominal words like darkness and silence, night and day; and the adjectives: white/light and black. Thus, words and phrases like 'a vibrant silence', 'a still night air', 'silence fell upon the earth', 'a deadly silence', 'solid massiveness of night', 'impenetrable darkness', 'darkness of the night', 'thick darkness', 'profound darkness', 'lump of darkness', 'as silent as death', 'circular and terrifying darkness', 'white head', and countless others punctuate his narrations. There seems to be a contrast between darkness and light in the first two parts of *Things Fall Apart.* Achebe's choice of such words as darkness, silence and light/white strengthens this suspicion. Answers to if there are contrasts and what they might be lie inside the novel. Whereas we see a different choice of words in the latter part of the novel, one wonders if Achebe alludes to the negative and positive impacts of the Igbo culture with these words. In the first part of the novel, Umuofia goes through different stages and events regarding their customs and tradition. Okonkwo was still in Umuofia and their daily life went on normally (before the British settled in the land). Within that social tranquillity, we take in a series of the clan's daily activities, including the 'atrocities' committed by some clan members against the gods and oracles of the land. It is possible that Achebe, with the word 'darkness,' might have been alluding to some of the traditions he considered bad, with the natives heeding to them without knowing the reasons behind their existence.

Traditions like the casting away of twin babies and sick people into the *evil forest*; the vicious discrimination against those termed *osu*; or the sacrificing of human heads, as in the case of Ikemefuna, etc. Seemingly, Achebe acknowledges that there are dark sides to the Igbo culture with his incessant use of darkness in the early parts of the novel. Parts of the culture did indeed appear to be in darkness, especially given that some of the elders of the clan kept questioning some dysfunctional beliefs. In chapter thirteen, we encounter Obierika, a man of thought, dismayed by the gods' punishment of Okonkwo over a crime he inadvertently committed.

> Obierika was a man who thought about things. When the will of the goddess had been done, he sat down in his obi and mourned his friend's calamity. Why should a man suffer so grievously for an offense he had committed inadvertently? But although he thought for a long time he found no answer. He was merely led into greater complexities. He remembered his wife's twin children, whom he had thrown away. What crime had they committed?[75]

Obierika's doleful musings, coupled with the lack of answers to the questions that tugged at his heart, make the dark, disturbing sides of the Igbo culture starker. Achebe's masterful fabrication of Obierika's pitiful circumstance induces the reader to ask the same question: 'What crime had they committed?' Not many Umuofians alive then even knew why or when some of those customs came to be, they abided by them without questioning their source for fear of the gods. Obierika, though, did not entirely agree with them. Prospecting further for the import of 'darkness' in Achebe's novel, one is led to think it had to do with Okonkwo's actions, and the calamities that trailed him from the very beginning to the end. Achebe could also have been referring to the future chaos in Umuofia upon the arrival of the white man when things began to fall apart in the clan. With the entry of the colonialists into Umuofia, several

---

75 Achebe, *Things Fall Apart*, 87.

unquestioned draconian traditions, which were really scarecrows and nothing more, started to lose adherents, until the clan became deeply polarized. It could also have been related to the oracle's submission to the elders when they consulted it in chapter fifteen: "the strange man would break their clan and spread destruction among them", and "that other white men were on their way. They were locusts, and, that the first man was their harbinger sent to explore the terrain."

The colonial mission, thus, was attributed to the arrival of the locusts to Umuofia, a development that was heralded in chapter seven.

> And then quite suddenly a shadow fell on the world, and the sun seemed hidden behind a thick cloud. …. At first, a fairly small swarm came. They were the harbingers sent to survey the land. And then appeared on the horizon a slowly moving mass like a boundless sheet of black cloud drifting towards Umuofia. Soon it covered half the sky, and the solid mass was now broken by tiny eyes of light like shining star dust. It was a tremendous sight, full of power and beauty. …. they settled on the roofs and covered the bare ground. Mighty tree branches broke away under them, and the whole country became the brown-earth colour of the vast, hungry swarm.[76]

In other words, Achebe uses locusts to symbolize the coming of the Europeans into Africa and stresses the impact of their coming on the culture. With this description ('a shadow on the world', and the 'thick cloud'), the arrival of the first small swarm prefigured 'darkness' in the story of Umuofia. The first white man that came, in reality, had been revealed as the harbinger sent to survey the land, and who was later followed by "a slowly moving mass like a boundless sheet of black cloud." That the "mighty tree branches broke away

---

76 Achebe, *Things Fall Apart*, 41.

under them" might have meant the rending of Igbo culture and tradition owing to the incursion of European colonialists. And finally, the white man's settlement in Africa occasioned the destruction of most African traditions.

A possible meaning to the frequent recurrence of 'silence' in Achebe's work could be taken from Uchendu's story about the mother kite and her daughter:

> Mother Kite once sent her daughter to bring food. She went, and brought back a duckling. 'You have done very well,' said Mother Kite to her daughter, 'but tell me, what did the mother of this duckling say when you swooped and carried its child away?' 'It said nothing,' replied the young kite. 'It just walked away.' 'You must return the duckling,' said Mother Kite. 'There is something ominous behind the silence.' And so Daughter Kite returned the duckling and took a chick instead. 'What did the mother of this chick do?' asked the old kite. 'It cried and raved and cursed me,' said the young kite. 'Then we can eat the chick,' said her mother. 'There is nothing to fear from someone who shouts.'[77]

It can likewise be said that there is something ominous behind the many 'silence' used in the narrator's description of the natural events in and around Umuofia. One guess could be that it portended that Umuofia would fall apart, would mourn. Another guess, is Okonkwo's tragic demise at the end of the novel. Another still, is the clan's silence and powerlessness before the white man, who went about desecrating and altering the people's sacred traditions. Whatever the case, the District Commissioner's silence and indifference towards the natives and their culture should not be ignored. The same District Commissioner's political interests, for which he sought to contribute a 'reasonable paragraph' on *The Pacification of*

---

77 Achebe, *Things Fall Apart*, 98-99.

the Primitive Tribes of the Lower Niger, alludes to the colonizer's keen-ness to silence the colonized. For him, Okonkwo's case was a good template for pacifying and silencing the natives, which in a way, recalls Kurtz interest in Conrad's *Heart of Darkness* when he wrote to the *International Society for the Suppression of Savage Customs* to "exterminate all the brutes".

Antithesis Within the Two Cultures in the Colonizing Mission

In *Things Fall Apart*, Achebe lets loose a diversity of characters through carefully crafted settings and scenes projecting a culture. Even though some characters appear rigid and ruthlessly pro-tradi-tion, they are quite peaceful and welcoming. For instance, conver-sations between Mr. Brown and Akunna (one of the greatest men of the clan) were carried on peacefully as if between two friends. In fact, with Mr. Brown, Achebe saved his work from projecting undue generalizations about the British in Igboland. On how Mr. Brown's character contrasted with Mr. Smith's, Achebe effectively bared his awareness that not all the missionaries and colonizers thought or behaved the same way. Mr. Brown and Akunna are the antithesis of Mr. Smith and Okonkwo in *Things Fall Apart*. Facing the same culture and circumstances, both Europeans reacted differently. "Mr. Smith openly condemned Mr. Brown's policy of compromise and accommodation and saw things as black and white. And black was evil. He was greatly distressed by the ignorance many of his flock showed even in such things as the trinity and sacraments." Mr. Smith was too desperate to replicate the culture and tradition of his home in the home of another, even appearing to be disappointed by their ignorance of Christianity. Achebe considered him a different kind of man from Mr. Brown: "He saw the world as a battlefield in which the children of light were locked in mortal conflict with the sons of darkness."

The District Commissioner is also a metaphor for the divide of the European colonizing contingent which considered colonization as a mission to impose their superior culture on inferior ones in Africa. Much of Achebe's works are a direct response to these elements, contending with their conclusions and enlightening their ignorance. Encumbered by his Christianity and eurocentrism, Mr. Smith failed even to see or observe the richness of the culture he sought so uncompromisingly to supplant. He did not possess the wisdom, or at least did not explore it, because that would have led him to adapt his own way of life to that of the Igbo society in which he found himself. Or, more likely, he felt too superior to condescend to the level of, as the District Commissioner puts it, "the primitive tribes of the lower Niger".

The Commissioner's imperialistic worldview was expressed in his address to the leading men of Umuofia thus: "We shall not do you any harm, if only you agree to cooperate with us. We have brought a peaceful administration to you and your people so that you may be happy." He said this after he had had them handcuffed and maltreated, which effectively demonstrated the agenda of the empire: dominion over the natives. Their promise of peace was a ploy to ensnare the natives and destroy the peace in Umuofia.

On the other hand, from their conversations, Mr. Brown and Akunna offered hope for a better understanding between the two cultures. According to the narrator, "whenever Mr. Brown went to that village he spent long hours with Akunna in his *obi* talking through an interpreter about religion. Neither of them succeeded in converting the other but they learned more about their different beliefs". This was a ray of hope for a civilized meeting and interaction of cultures, if only it were nurtured. With Mr. Brown spending long hours with Akunna, it is clear that both men respected each other's essence and beliefs. No one condemned the other; instead, they both tried to learn more about their different beliefs. They tolerated each other by listening intently as each talked about his religious and cultural beliefs.

By emphasizing Mr. Brown's studious visits to Akunna, Achebe asserts that he, who did not pay attention to the natives' ways, was wrong. Invariably, Mr. Smith. The two friends gained deep insights into their religious beliefs, to the extent that some connections began to appear. For instance, Akunna once asked Mr. Brown during one of his visits: "You say that there is one supreme God who made heaven and earth, we also believe in Him and call Him *Chukwu*. He made the entire world and the other gods." The Igbo tradition taught *Chukwu*, while Christianity taught God; both were regarded as supreme and believed in very similar ways. Thus, a self-immersion in the beliefs of the other might have helped them to understand they merely had different means of revering the same God. What the missionaries thought fetish and pagan were actually the ways in which the Igbos demonstrated their faith and devotion to the supreme God. The carved woods they used were not idols but instruments through which they communicated with their God, an approach that is not alien to Christendom. According to Chief Edochie, "the precolonial Igbo used carved pieces of woods because they considered it inanimate and incorruptible, human beings are prone to corruption and can easily be bribed." Akunna, likewise, attempted an explanation to Mr. Brown:

> The head of your church is in your country. He has sent you here as his messenger. And you have also appointed your own messengers and servants. Or let me take another example, the District Commissioner. He is sent by your king." [...] "Your queen sends her messenger, the District Commissioner. He finds that he cannot do the work alone and so he appoints *kotma* to help him. It is the same

with God, or *Chukwu*. He appoints the smaller gods to help Him
because His work is too great for one person.[78]

With his emphasis on the quality of Mr. Brown's personality,
Achebe helps his readers to isolate Mr. Smith's character as the
unfortunate tragedy of one man and not of a nation. He showed
a different character of the white man, a reasonable character. He
did not generalize everything about the colonial mission. On this
occasion, it was obvious to the reader that Achebe recognized the
positive impact of the colonial administration on Igbo culture and
valued some aspects of the western culture.

On the Igbo front, the antithesis of Okonkwo was Akunna, a
well-respected leader of the clan of Umuofia. As a forward thinker,
Akunna had considered the value that education would bring to
Umuofia long before the Europeans gained traction with its proposal to the natives. For this reason, he had his son educated by
the missionaries, thereby using his family as an example to others.
He was respectful of other people's points of view, especially when
it came to religion and beliefs. He served as a bridge between the
colonial regime and the people of Umuofia, not opening the door
entirely to a barrage of western influence and, at the same time,
not shutting it from the entry of new beneficial ideas. Just like Mr.
Brown, Akunna portrayed the other side of the Igbo society that
was open to dialogue, was understanding, and was willing to adapt.
In his debates with Mr. Brown, he formulated a rational defence of
his style of worship and traced some similarities between his religious belief and that of the Christian missionaries. If Mr. Brown had
maintained, after his sufficient exposure to Akunna's logic, that his
beliefs were superior, then at least he would have learned from their
conversations that a frontal attack on the culture and beliefs of the
natives would do more harm than good to his mission of religious

---

78 Achebe, *Things Fall Apart*, 127.

conversion. Indeed, it was based on the information he obtained
from their conversations that Mr. Brown devised how best to inter-
act with the people of Umuofia. As a result, he did not directly
challenge them, like Mr. Smith would do, but he coaxed them into
bringing their children to his school and, from thence, furthered his
missionary project.

Okonkwo was different from Akunna. Like Mr. Smith, his western counterpart, Okonkwo was an embodiment of, not only of the
Igbo culture, but also of the African traditional worldview. He adored
being considered a strong, uncompromising man. In fact, he was
popularly called the 'Roaring Flame', or the flaming fire. Compared to
Akunna, he was a rigid fellow who would go to great lengths, including killing his own son, to preserve tradition. For him, being tolerant
and affectionate were signs of weakness that made one appear more
like a woman than a man. Okonkwo represented moral rectitude and
the preservation of Umuofia's cultural heritage. He was a symbol of
anti-colonialism, as he never fancied any contact with the colonial
regime. Ultimately, what he lived for, he also died for.

Okonkwo, an Archetype of the Igbo Man

To the question on whether Okonkwo is a representation or an
archetype of the Igbo man, Edochie opined that Okonkwo was but
a concept. "*Things Fall Apart* essentially was a conflict between a
new order represented by the white man, the imperialist, and ours
represented by Okonkwo. Okonkwo represents the essence, the sacrosanctity of the Igbo culture. The white man was out there to use
his own culture to supplant the Igbo culture and Okonkwo resisted
it." Having played Okonkwo in the movie adaptation of the novel,
Edochie prefigured Okonkwo as a projection of the black man's
epic resistance to the invasion of his own culture by white values.
He further said that, like Okonkwo,

Igbo people value honour a lot. Rather than a man to remain alive and witness shame, he will prefer to hang himself and that was exactly what Okonkwo did. Okonkwo was born at a time when our culture was being invaded by the white culture. There was a clash between the cultures, but then, Okonkwo was conservative, he wanted to make sure that the essence, the core of his own culture was preserved whereas the colonists were intent on ensuring that they forced their own culture on the Igbos and that led to a clash between the two cultures. Achebe mirrored that situation perfectly well in *Things Fall Apart* and this made the novel a very successful portrayal of the Igbo culture, illustrating the pride of the Igbo man who is very proud of his culture and, is fulfilling some aspect of his existence that in a way should be emulated by other cultures. The Igbo man, like Okonkwo, is very creative, always obsessed with the desire to conquer his environment. He does not believe that the environment offers challenges that are insurmountable. Achebe did a very successful portrayal of what the Igbo-man represents when it comes to defending his culture and tradition in *Things Fall Apart*.[79]

Edochie referred to Shakespeare's *Henry VI*: "if it be a crime to value honour, then I am the most offending slave alive". This, he said, propels the entire life of the Igbo man like that of Okonkwo. According to him, "the entire story, Achebe, Edochie (as the main character in the movie) and Okonkwo in the novel, all insisted on projecting 'moral rectitude.' Okonkwo found himself in a situation where he had to represent a conflict. This is Igbo culture represented by Okonkwo, and he wanted to make sure that our own culture was preserved. He offered resistance to the invasion of his culture. The Igbo would not mind existing side by side with whatever the white man represented but the white man wanted to make sure that he supplanted the Igbo culture, and this is what Okonkwo resisted.

79 Edochie, interview.

Therefore, his life was not a tragedy and it would be very awkward to view it that way. Again, he did not, in any way, signal the collapse of the Igbo culture. On the contrary, it reinforced our conviction in our traditional values. Okonkwo is not a failure; his demise was not a tragedy but a self-sacrifice. He was willing to die for what he believed in and that is Honor."[80]

Okonkwo's Misfortunes

Okonkwo was well known for his bravery and determination, and he was loved in the clan for his fame. In the latter paragraphs of the second chapter, Achebe sheds more light on the personality of Okonkwo by describing him as a man who ruled his household with a heavy hand. "His wives, especially the youngest, lived in perpetual fear of his fiery temper, and so did his little children. Perhaps down in his heart Okonkwo was not a cruel man. However, his whole life was dominated by fear, the fear of failure and of weakness... It was the fear of himself, lest he should be found to resemble his father." He was ruled by the fear of being thought weak and so would rather not be gentle or idle.

As a committed Igbo man, he wanted his household to mirror his convictions by being strong and hardworking. But, unfortunately for him, his son, Nwoye, threw him a curveball by looking more like his grandfather, Unoka. Okonkwo's dream for Nwoye was lofty; he had wanted the boy to take after him and expressed his disappointment when he said, with reference to Nwoye, "I will not have a son who cannot hold up his head in the gathering of the clan. I would sooner strangle him with my own hands." To add to his disappointment, Nwoye went after the Christian missionaries.

Okonkwo's father, Unoka, was ill-fated. Misfortune followed him about, even to his death. He was not given a proper burial and

---

80 Ibid.

had no grave of his own. In fact, his impending death by swelling signaled a bad omen; an abomination; hence, he was thrown into the evil forest and was left alone to die a miserable death. The image of his father haunted Okonkwo to the point that he came across like one running from his own shadow. He dreaded any traces of Unoka in himself, and so worked extra hard to establish himself as a contrasting image of his father. His determination notwithstanding, Okonkwo still could not delete the fact of his father's shameful existence and pathetic demise. In the Igbo culture, the foundation for a man's greatness was the quality of the burial he accorded his father. His father neither had a first burial nor a second one; worse still, he did not have a grave. There is a fitting Igbo adage for Okonkwo's circumstance: no matter how hard one tries to cure a madman, he could never remove the constant lamentation that would have become a habit. In other words, there would always be traces of Unoka in Okonkwo. Hard as Okonkwo tried, he was never going to reach the highest echelons of relevance and respect in the clan.

In the first chapters of *Things Fall Apart*, Okonkwo is seen excelling in the clan and being talked about by everyone. He was revered, amongst other things, for defeating a renowned wrestler — Amalinze the Cat — in a bout. With two barns, three wives, and many children, Okonkwo was quite accomplished. However, this did not completely erase the fear within him, of being associated with his failure of a father, Unoka. This fear turned to dread the more his reputation grew, eventually leading to his destruction in the end. Like his father, Okonkwo did not receive a burial, having committed suicide — an abomination in the land. Alas, his bitter end did not entirely come as a surprise; from the beginning to the end, his life oscillated between good fortune and misfortune. We will examine just how.

Firstly, from the beginning, readers come to know Okonkwo as a violent man, a wife-beater. He beats up his wife, Ojiugo, during the sacred week of peace. "He walked back to his obi to await

Ojiugo's return. And when she returned he beat her very heavily. In his anger, he had forgotten that it was the Week of Peace. His first two wives ran out in great alarm, pleading with him that it was the sacred week. But Okonkwo was not the man to stop beating somebody halfway through, not even for fear of a goddess." He broke the law of the land. As was the custom in Umuofia, the sacred week of peace was dedicated to the goddess of the land. It was a week of atonement and supplication for the earth goddess to grant them increase and abundance.

Okonkwo, therefore, effectively stood in the way of the community's aspirations. As Ezeani put it, Okonkwo's evil act was enough to ruin the entire clan, and cause the earth goddess to refuse to give an increase to Umuofia. One would expect that Okonkwo, who was very preservative of his culture, would not break the law of the land in such a manner. But, even after being reminded that it was the sacred week of peace, he did not stop. This cast a shadow over his faithfulness to the clan and reverence for the gods of the land.

Secondly, Okonkwo slew a lad that called him father. "As the man who had cleared his throat drew up and raised his machete, Okonkwo looked away. He heard the blow. The pot fell and broke in the sand. He heard Ikemefuna cry, "My father, they have killed me!" as he ran towards him. Dazed with fear, Okonkwo drew his machete and cut him down. He was afraid of being thought weak." Per Obierika's estimation, Okonkwo's slaying of Ikemefuna was an abomination of epic proportions, one that was capable of leading to the wiping out of his entire family. "What you have done", said Obierika to his friend, "will not please the Earth. It is the kind of action for which the goddess wipes out whole families." In retrospect, Obierika's words resound like a prophecy. Okonkwo's family did suffer some form of wiping out. Nwoye, his son, abandoned his father's traditional beliefs and went after the Christian missionaries. Okonkwo himself was forced into exile in Mbanta. While there, his family was displaced and humiliated by the gods of the land. Eventually, he dies quite tragically. All his life's work came to naught: his good name was tarnished, his end was abominable, and he had no grave. He succumbed to the fear that haunted him all his life. He met with his destiny on the very road he took to avoid it. In the end, he was his father's son.

The third misfortune that befell Okonkwo occurred during the funeral of Ezeudu. As the traditional farewell dance went on, his gun exploded, and a shrapnel hit and killed Ezeudu's sixteen-year-old son. This was at the climax of the funeral rites:

> The drums and the dancing began again and reached fever-heat. Darkness was around the corner, and the burial was near. Guns fired the last salute and the cannon rent the sky. Then from the centre of the delirious fury came a cry of agony and shouts of horror. It was as if a spell had been cast. All was silent. In the centre of the crowd a boy lay in a pool of blood. It was the dead man's sixteen-year-old son, who with his brothers and half-brothers had been dancing the traditional farewell to their father. Okonkwo's gun had exploded and a piece of iron had pierced the boy's heart.[81]

The reader gathers that violent deaths were not new in Umuofia, but that one like the death of Ezeudu's son had never happened before. It was strange, suggestive that Okonkwo's fate was unusual. Different. When he infringed the law of the week of peace, it was similarly said that no man had ever beaten his wife during the sacred observance. In the case of Ezeudu's son, it was clearly an accident but, still, there were consequences. Following the incident, Okonkwo and his family fled Umuofia for seven years, because it was a crime against the earth goddess to kill a clansman.

Okonkwo's fourth misfortune would come from his son, Nwoye, who abandoned the ways of his forebears and went after the

---

81 Achebe, *Things Fall Apart*, 86.

Christian missionaries. Nwoye denounced Okonkwo as his father: "How is your father?' Obierika asked, not knowing what else to say. 'I don't know. He is not my father' said Nwoye, unhappily." It hurt Okonkwo, even if he did not show it. Nwoye, along with other converts to Christianity, caused the clan to fall apart. Okonkwo pondered:

> To abandon the gods of one's father and go about with a lot of effeminate men clucking like old hens was the very depth of abomination. Suppose when he died all his male children decided to follow Nwoye's steps and abandon their ancestors? Okonkwo felt a cold shudder run through him at the terrible prospect, like the prospect of annihilation. He saw himself and his forefathers crowding round their ancestral shrine waiting in vain for worship and sacrifice and finding nothing but ashes of bygone days, and his children there while praying to the white man's god.[82]

At this thought, Okonkwo "sighed heavily, and as if in sympathy, the smoldering log also sighed. And immediately, Okonkwo's eyes were opened and he saw the whole matter clearly. Living fire begets cold, impotent ash. He sighed again, deeply."

The fifth misfortune of Okonkwo would be the killing of the court messenger sent by the District Commissioner to stop the clan's gathering:

> Okonkwo confronted the head messenger, trembling with hate, unable to utter a word. [...] In that brief moment the world seemed to stand still, waiting. There was utter silence. The men of Umuofia were merged into the mute backcloth of trees and giant creepers, waiting.' 'In a flash Okonkwo drew his machete. The messenger

---

82 Achebe, *Things Fall Apart*, 108.

crouched to avoid the blow. It was useless. Okonkwo's machete descended twice and the man's head lay beside his uniformed body.[83]

Again, the abomination of killing a clansman. It was unnecessary, especially because the gods were capable of fighting their own cause if and when slighted. Beyond killing a clansman, Okonkwo took the law into his own hands by not allowing the gods to avenge their cause. Therefore, he brought another calamity upon himself, culminating in what some scholars call the tragedy of Okonkwo — his death by suicide.

However, considering the grave and violent errors of his ways, it is hard to agree with the scholars that his suicide is a tragedy. Okonkwo did not heed his maternal uncle, Uchendu's, advice given while he was on exile in Mbanta. Uchendu had spoken to him about the need to be patient with life when he said, "Do you know how many children I have buried—children I begot in my youth and strength? Twenty-two. I did not hang myself, and I am still alive." When the calamities arising from his obstinacy came to a head, Okonkwo did hang himself. Many scholars contend that Okonkwo's misfortune is his agreement with his *chi*, the apparent phenomenon is Okonkwo's interaction with non-physical beings.

His life is undoubtedly not his alone, but something he shares with his *chi*. As much as he tried to live by the Igbos' belief that *onye kwe chi ya ekwe* (if one agrees, his chi will also agree with him), it appeared that the decision was not his alone to take. Thus, his eventual misfortune is not attributable to his humanity alone, but to his *chi's* destiny as well. The narrator suggests, after all, that it was possible that Okonkwo's personal god was not made for great things.[84] Okpala opines that Okonkwo's "life is a fluctuation between joy and sorrow. His agreement with his *chi* resonates in his success and achievements, and in his

---

83 Achebe, *Things Fall Apart*, 143.
84 Jude Chudi Okpala, "Igbo Metaphysics in Chinua Achebe's *Things Fall Apart*," *Callaloo* Vol. 25, no. 2 (Spring, 2002): 562.

people's recognition of his integrity." Okonkwo was presented in two different lights; even though he and his *chi* were in one accord, it must not be forgotten that "he infringed the laws of the land: he broke the week of peace; he killed Ikemefuna, etc."[85]

These events made Okonkwo's fate very ambiguous in relation to his *chi*. Recall that Ezeani and Obierika warned him about the gravity of his actions against the gods of the land. This "shows that Okonkwo's agreement with his *chi* is dissipated; his action is not in accordance with the will of the gods, nor even with the will of his people" (Okpala). Agreeably, as argued by Opkala, "it would be improper to say that Okonkwo's life represents a contradiction; his life represents one who has arrogated to himself the power of the non-physical being and who has forgotten the power of *chi*. Okonkwo excised himself from that complex community, from the interconnection of things, to pursue his aggrandized individual ego."

Hence, it could be said that, contrary to representing a contradiction, he at times contributed to his misfortune by his own personal will. Since the Igbos believed that a man's life is not his alone, but something he shared with his *chi*, it follows that Okonkwo's decision to commit suicide was taken in one accord with his *chi*. However, if his *chi* wanted his death to preserve the land, it would not have allowed it to occur in a manner that was considered abominable in the land.

Again, he could have allowed his *chi* to avenge its cause given that it was not the Igbo custom to fight for the gods. Under this circumstance, yet another Igbo belief could apply: *onye bute chi ya uzo, ogbagbue onwe ya n'oso*, a man who runs ahead of his god, will run himself to death. Okonkwo's cup was full, and, by hanging himself, he committed a further abomination against the earth goddess, on account of which he was not to be buried by his clansmen but by men of another clan. As explained by Okpala, "to die without

---

85 Ibid.

a burial is the worst thing that could happen to an Igbo person because burial suggests both a physical and spiritual transaction with the ancestors; burial sets one off on the ancestral journey among the spirits. To die without one implies that you have lost all connections with the ancestors, with the people, and the land." Okonkwo lost every connection with his clan and with the gods. Sacrifices were even made to cleanse the land he desecrated and to appease the gods. It is unclear if the men from another clan buried him in Umuofia or elsewhere. But we hear the District Commissioner order his chief messenger to bring Okonkow's body along with the other people to the court. If he was buried, no reference was made to his grave. It was not important. Following his death, we only hear Obierika talk about sacrifices to appease the gods of the land and nothing more. Okonkwo lost the continual ancestral train of reverence which he longed earnestly to receive from his children while he was alive. His place in Umuofia's folklore remains uncertain. However, being one of the greatest men of Umuofia, as Obierika said, Okonkwo may have been restored to the clan's hierarchy of ancestors by the sacrifices of appeasement offered by his clansmen.

Okonkwo's Demise: A Tragedy and Collapse of the Igbo Culture?

There is a twofold approach to interpreting Okonkwo's demise in *Things Fall Apart*. Firstly, as argued by some scholars, his death could be considered a tragedy. Secondly, as argued by Edochie and some others, it could be seen as heroic. Richard Begam in his essay, *Achebe's sense of an ending,* elaborated the question of closure and ending in *Things Fall Apart*, and he argued that the novel "resists the idea of a single or simple resolution" and that it provides three distinct endings, that is, "three different ways of reading the events that conclude the novel."

According to him, the first ending is a heroic tragedy, which centers on "Okonkwo's killing of the court messenger, his failed attempt to rouse his people to action, and his subsequent suicide."[86] Therefore, he equated Okonkwo's demise to the collapse of Igbo culture based on the idea that Okonkwo's destiny was linked to that of his people. He was associated with the founder of their clan who engaged a spirit of the wild in a fight for seven days and seven nights. In Begam's words, "Achebe illustrates how Okonkwo has come to personify the destiny of his community, extending from its earliest origins to its final destruction"[87] and that his failures (his destruction) are, in essence, virtues carried to an extreme.

Begam's second ending is what he calls the irony of the novel. In his opinion, "by ironically undermining the perspective of the District Commissioner, by exposing the latter's personal ignorance and political interest" (when the District Commissioner said at the end that perhaps he could write not a 'whole chapter' but a 'reasonable paragraph' on Okonkwo, and in his idea of the *pacification of the Lower Niger*), Achebe in a way, "seeks to confront and finally to discredit the entire discourse of colonialism, those quasi-historical, quasi-anthropological writings that have treated Africa as nothing more than a foil to Europe, and a place of negations."[88]

In the third ending, Begam views Okonkwo's demise as a modern tragedy that portrays the perplexing and ambiguous relationship between the postcolonial writer and its own history. The third ending shows that the lines between the heroic and ironic do not always line up perfectly. Many critics have argued that Okonkwo's death was a tragedy, given the fact that he hanged himself; and his demise has been associated with the collapse of Igbo culture. For instance, Begam suggests that "Achebe's sense of an ending is intimately bound up with his sense of cultural loss."

---

86 Richard Begam. "Achebe's sense of an ending: History and tragedy in *Things Fall Apart*," *Studies in the Novel*, 29, no.2 (Fall 1997): 398.
87 Begam, "Achebe's sense of an ending," 399.
88 Ibid, 403.

Having seen Begam's standpoint, one thing that is particularly noteworthy, according to him, is that the novel does not privilege one of the alternative endings. "In other words, we are not meant to choose from among three possible endings, but to read all of them, as it were, simultaneously and palimpsestically."[89] Most critics agreed and argued in tune with Begam, but it would be good to look at it from another perspective: that Okonkwo's demise was not in any way the demise of Igbo culture.

With what is said above, it will be interesting to look at it from the perspective of Edochie and Afigbo. Contrary to Begam's argument on Achebe's sense of cultural loss, Afigbo argues that it would be a "gross exaggeration to say that Igbo society and culture disintegrated or collapsed under colonial rule for, to a greater extent than has so far been recognized, the Igbos have sought to use institutions and techniques acquired through the link with the outside world established by colonial rule to maintain those values and styles of life which are intrinsic to their separate identity."[90] In like manner, Edochie, in a recent interview, held that "Okonkwo's death in *Things Fall Apart* was not in any way a tragedy, neither was it the collapse of the Igbo culture. Unfortunately, many scholars see it as tragic but it is not."

This study agrees with Afigbo and Edochie that Igbo culture did not collapse under colonial rule, and, Okonkwo's demise did not prefigure the destruction of the Igbo culture because the culture and identity still exist in today's South-Eastern Nigeria. Okonkwo is a hero and a moral flag bearer of his culture and therefore a relevant character in the Igbo society. Okonkwo is a hero even though with some converging viewpoints. His indomitable spirit and courageous responses to various situations in his life stood him out. He held his clan in high regard and gave everything to preserve it. He stood for and defended his clan's ideals. Therefore, his death was heroic, not

---

89 Begam, "Achebe's sense of an ending," 406.
90 Afigbo, *Ropes of Sand*, 284.

tragic. He subdued himself to uphold his land because he could not bear to see the clan fall.

Okonkwo saw Nwoye's affiliation with the missionaries not only as a personal calamity but also as a threat to the entire clan. Achebe keeps readers' focused on Okonkwo by isolating him from the mass of his clans people. The more readers know him, the more likely they pity him. Even the natural world surrounding him seemed to pity him as well, with smoldering logs sighing when he sighed. "And immediately Okonkwo's eyes were opened and he saw the whole matter clearly. Living fire begets cold, impotent ash. He sighed again, deeply." Things began to fall apart in Umuofia when some brothers abandoned common chores or sport to follow their white visitors. Sons denied their fathers; and sons of the land began to contradict the gods of the land. Things began to fall apart when the elders, searching for solutions to their problems, consulted the oracle and were told that the strange man would break their clan and spread destruction among them; when a good number of the clansmen joined the white man to kill their fellow clansmen. Things fell apart.

Okonkwo was a distinguished clansman. A man of valor, his love for and dedication to his clan made him one with it. Aware that the white man had hanged a clansman who killed a missionary, he decided to take his own life rather than die in a stranger's hands. That he had killed a messenger working for the District Commissioner was also a factor. He embodied Umuofia's ideals, yet he had his flaws. He was a sucker for perfection, and this led him to extremism. His flaws reflected the imperfections in the order through which Umuofia recreated itself. Achebe, an Igbo man, was not one to only glorify his tribe or continent. He presented the two sides of the coin as far as Igbo culture was concerned.

Some scholars opine that Okonkwo would have made a fine ally for the colonial regime if he weren't so obsessed with his culture. His misfortune, therefore, they say, is attributable to the fact that the old order he cherished was ill-fated, and a new order sure to come. Opkala's opinion differs; according to him "Okonkwo's misfortune, which culminates in his suicide, cannot only be rationalized as such, for as his situation is underscored in the text, it is obvious that his personal god or *chi* was not made for great things."[91] What he did was, in effect, not the only remedy in such a situation; and it should not be forgotten that his *chi* played a vital role in his life as was the Igbo belief. Agreeably, it would be improper to assert that Okonkwo's life implies a contradiction; His life represents a person who has forgotten about the power of his *chi* and has delegated to himself the power of non-physical beings. Okonkwo removed himself from the interconnectedness of that complex community in order to further his own ambitions.[92]

The scholars who hold the opinion that Okonkwo aligned with an outgoing order and so had to die were wrong for two reasons. Firstly, today's Igbo society is a beneficiary of many positives of the British culture. At no point did the Igbo culture exit the stage for the British; it continued to exist alongside it and became the richer for it. Secondly, all cultures are eclectic and evolve over time. Cultures go from primitive to exotic and on to dominant. Or the reverse. In this case, it is always inevitable that a culture gives up something of its own to assimilate better things from others. In the case of Okonkwo, the Igbo culture simply made room in order to receive. Hence, his death would not be termed a tragedy, but a personal sacrifice made for the greater good. Again, the Igbo culture did not collapse; most of the cultural values represented in the fictional clan of Umuofia still exist in today's Igbo society. Cultural values like negotiation of marriage, burial ceremony, clan gathering, naming ceremony, title taking, child visitation, the issue of primogeniture, etc. have all remained intact.

In the last chapter of the novel, Obierika renders an explanation

---

91 Okpala, "Igbo Metaphysics in Chinua Achebe's *Things Fall Apart*," 562.
92 Ibid.

to the District Commissioner on the implications of Okonkwo's action:

> "It is against our custom," said one of the men. "It is an abomination for a man to take his own life. It is an offense against the Earth, and a man who commits it will not be buried by his clansmen. His body is evil, and only strangers may touch it. That is why we ask your people to bring him down, because you are strangers." "Will you bury him like any other man?" asked the Commissioner. "We cannot bury him. Only strangers can. We shall pay your men to do it. When he has been buried we will then do our duty by him. We shall make sacrifices to cleanse the desecrated land." Obierika, who had been gazing steadily at his friend's dangling body, turned suddenly to the District Commissioner and said ferociously: "That man was one of the greatest men in Umuofia. You drove him to kill himself and now he will be buried like a dog.[93]

Gender in *Things Fall Apart*

The relationship between the genders in *Things Fall Apart* is quite intriguing. Achebe presented readers with two different perspectives. The first is the quasi-representation of a masculine nationalist tradition, which is evident in the novel's setting. The second is the ceding of primary roles ranging from economic, and socio-political to spiritual roles to women. In other words, Achebe presented women as innovators and emissaries of a new order, while presenting the men as the center of social order in the clan.

Umuofia was a patriarchal society that applauded masculinist exhibitions. Women were not granted the privilege to participate in some social functions. For instance, title-taking was exclusively

---

93 Achebe, *Things Fall Apart*, 145.

for men; women were not allowed to attend men's gatherings, and when they did attend, they played only passive roles. Women never questioned the gods and never asked questions about the most powerful secret cults in the clan. Women were forbidden from seeing the inside of *egwugwu*'s hut. During festive periods, they scrubbed and painted the external walls of the hut under the supervision of men.

Osei-Nyame Kwadwo was spot on with his verdict in his *Representations of Gender and Tradition in Things Fall Apart,* that "Achebe's text links and identifies power and authority with masculinity. Umuofia's masculine traditions are heralded and celebrated, and the representation of masculine ideology is progressively played out mainly through the representation of the legendary Okonkwo and his obsessive pursuit of the fulfillment of personal power and recognition within the clan."[94]

Indeed, *Things Fall Apart* began with the praise of Okonkwo's manly qualities. His fame was built on masculinity. He was "well known throughout the nine villages and even beyond." Known, not for anything else, but for his strength, grit, and possessions — which included wives and children. At eighteen, he had already brought honor to his village by outwitting Amalinze the Cat in a wrestling contest. The high praise he received owed much to the reputation of the man he conquered.

To give context to Okonkwo's feat, fresh renditions of Amalinze's greatness as a wrestler rent the air. Mention was also made of the founder of the town who engaged a spirit of the wild in a bout for seven days and seven nights. These made it clear that Umuofia was a clan of warriors and was feared by other clans. The description of Okonkwo in the first chapter of the novel painted a picture of a powerful fellow that was both feared and admired simultaneously.

---

94 Osei-Nyame Kwadwo, "Chinua Achebe Writing Culture: Representations of gender and Tradition in *Things Fall Apart*," *Research in African Literature*, Vol. 30, no. 2 (Summer 1999): 150.

However, tall as he stood amid his records and achievements, his imperfections also glared at him, he was said to have a slight stammer and a raging temper.

On more than one occasion, he was described as the roaring flame. He had no tolerance for and was impatient with unsuccessful and lazy men, one of whom was his own father. The only emotion he ever showed in public was anger. To him, showing affection was a sign of weakness, whereas all he wanted to showcase was strength. Because of this, he treated Ikemefuna the same way he treated everybody else — with a heavy hand. Umuofia's hegemonic masculinist culture dictated that, for a man to gain social acknowledgment, he must subdue his non-masculine features and project the masculine ones. For this reason, therefore, Okonkwo's family became the victim of his attempts to show himself as manly. He was stern and heavy-handed, he did not express affection, and did not tolerate their little failings, lest he be taught a lesser man than he would like to be seen. He confused gentleness for weakness and this "upsets the sexual equilibrium that maintains a delicate balance between male values and female and maternal ones in any society." (Osei-Nyame)

In Okonkwo's estimation, rather than show affection, men should instead work to earn fear and respect by seeking fame, greatness, and personal achievements. His dislike for his father, Unoka, came from this mindset. Effeminate men like Unoka undermined Umuofia's reputation as a patriarchy and a clan of warriors; hence, they were merely tolerated. They were subjected to social and public shame, and considered onlookers and second-class citizens.

It was every boy's ambition to avoid that company, and this made Umuofia a place of stiff competition among the men. Okonkwo feared for Nwoye, because he did not seem interested in the heated race that other ambitious young men were in. He often had Nwoye and Ikemefuna "sit with him in his obi, and he told them stories of the land — masculine stories of violence and bloodshed. Nwoye knew that it was right to be masculine and to be violent, but somehow he still preferred the stories that his mother used to tell, and which she no doubt still told to her younger children — stories of the tortoise and his wily ways, and of the bird *eneke-nti-oba,* who challenged the whole world to a wrestling contest and was finally thrown by the cat." Okonkwo disliked it when he saw Nwoye exhibiting 'feminine' traits, like listening to stories he believed were meant for foolish women and children. The traces of negative emotion he felt after slaying Ikemefuna perturbed him greatly that he sat pondering: "When did you become a shivering old woman, you who are known in all the nine villages for your valour in war? How can a man who has killed five men in battle fall to pieces because he has added a boy to their number? Okonkwo, you have become a woman indeed." It was not enough that he did not show emotions in public, he also did not want to acknowledge it in his thoughts.

Derided as he was in Umuofia, Unoka still had a fine, meaningful existence. In the fourth paragraph of chapter one, he was described as a peaceful man who brought joy to others with his flute. "He was very good on his flute, and his happiest moments were the two or three moons after the harvest when the village musicians brought down their instruments, hung above the fireplace. Unoka would play with them, his face beaming with blessedness and peace. Unoka loved the good hire and the good fellowship". Though not a manly art by Umuofia's standards, Unoka was at his best when he played his flute. Umuofia did not value gentle and meek men; they termed them women. The idea was that women are weak, and so not much was expected of them.

Being pro-Umuofia by protecting its values, Okonkwo was the archetype of a true clansman. He lorded over his household in the manner that the clan prescribed; women and children were to have no say, all they did was obey. He despised his father and was also crossed with his son, Nwoye, for being like his grandfather, Unoka. At the very least, Nwoye was a son; very little was said of Okonkwo's daughters, except one, Ezinma, whom Okonkwo wished was a boy. "She should have been a boy, he thought." As a result, we see him turn down Ezimma's proposal to help him carry his chair to the clan's gathering. She was a girl, and chairs were only meant to be carried to social gatherings by boys. Gender equity in Umuofia was non-existent; Okonkwo beat his wives over trivial issues, spoke to them harshly, and didn't tolerate the insolence of having them speak while he spoke.

In precolonial Igbo society, men were encouraged to marry as many wives as they deemed possible. Women only had a passive voice in the men's world that was Umuofia. Achebe further illustrated Umuofia's masculine hegemony by legitimizing men's dominant position in society and justifying the subjugation of women and women-like men. In fact, this is in effect in the second chapter of the novel when the men of Umuofia gathered to take a decision on neighbouring Mbaino: "In the morning the market place was full. There must have been about ten thousand men there, all talking in low voices. At last, Ogbuefi Ezeugo stood up in the midst of them and bellowed four good times, 'Umuofia kwenu' and on each occasion, he faced a different direction and seemed to push the air with a clenched fist. And ten thousand men answered "Yaa!" each time. Then there was perfect silence." The emphasis was on "ten thousand men," which was repeated two different times.

Umuofia conferred an unquestionable authority on men by reserving a self-representative democracy and exclusively vesting them with judicial powers. In this male-centered social order where women were only functional to men, once a man paid his wife's dowry, he received total authority to do as he pleased with her. Therefore, Okonkwo was within his rights to yell at and beat his wives, as he did during the sacred week of peace and during preparations for the New Yam Festival.

> …Okonkwo knew she was not speaking the truth. He walked back to his obi to await Ojiugo's return. And when she returned he beat

her very heavily. In his anger, he had forgotten that it was the Week of Peace. His first two wives ran out in great alarm pleading with him that it was the sacred week." […] "And then the storm burst. Okonkwo, who had been walking about aimlessly in his compound in suppressed anger, suddenly found an outlet. "Who killed this banana tree?" he asked. A hush fell on the compound immediately. "Who killed this tree? Or are you all deaf and dumb? As a matter of fact, the tree was very much alive. Okonkwo's second wife had merely cut a few leaves off it to wrap some food, and she said so. Without further argument, Okonkwo gave her a sound beating and left her and her only daughter weeping. Neither of the other wives dared to interfere beyond an occasional and tentative, "It is enough, Okonkwo," pleaded from a reasonable distance.[95]

In chapter eight of *Things Fall Apart*, Achebe describes the Igbo traditional marriage rite. It was striking how Akueke's suitor and relatives "surveyed" her young body to assure themselves that she was beautiful and ripe. In the early Igbo community, young women were negotiated for like commodities in the local market by their suitors. In the case of Akueke, her bride price was beaten down from thirty to twenty bags of cowries. Women were not allowed to be part of the negotiation; they only came in afterward to serve and entertain the visitors.

Uzowulu illustrated this further when he presented the case with his wife to the *Evil Forest* and the other *egwugwus*. "That woman standing there is my wife, Mgbafo. I married her with my money and my yams. I do not owe my in-laws anything. I owe them no yams. I owe them no coco-yams." It appeared that women had no rights because they had been paid for.

This situation notwithstanding, Achebe reserves the future for women, listing them as flag-bearers of a new and balanced social

---

95 Achebe, *Things Fall Apart*, 23.

order in the Igbo society. They were innovators and incubators of the future, gradually sowing in their children the seeds of change through daily storytelling. The stories were laced with wisdom, the sort that negated the relegation of women and the building of society on the brute strength of prideful men. Yet, in this male-dominated society, some women stood out. Women like Chielo (the priestess of the gods), Ekwefi, and Ezinma. These women fearlessly opposed the masculinist authority of Umuofia. They undermined the great Okonkwo when they embarked on their heroic journey to *Agbala*. His own journey proved futile and dented the clan's patriarchal authority. A few days later, Okonkwo was forced into exile with his three women.

Chielo's encounter with Ekwefi and Ezinma prefigured the dethronement of patriarchy in Umuofia. Additionally, Ekwefi found rare courage to disregard and even challenge Okonkwo's orders by continuing to give Ezinma eggs. According to Osei-Nyame, it is clear that Ekwefi and Ezinma "partially denied Okonkwo some of the authority he seeks to wield over them by conspiring to ensure that Ezinma eats eggs despite Okonkwo's threat to beat Ekwefi if she continues to let Ezinma have the delicacy."[96]

Furthermore, as Ezinma narrated a certain tale about how the cat and the tortoise wrestled with the yam, she implied the conquest of the yam — a symbolic food commodity. Yam represented the masculine tradition of not just Umuofia, but the Igbos as a whole. Ezinma's tale of the cat and the tortoise wrestling with the yam prefigured the questioning of masculine superiority in the clan. Unsurprisingly, just before the arrival of Chielo, the priestess of *Agbala*, Ezinma was on the verge of telling her story; a tale where the cat and the tortoise are presented as an incarnation of the feminist features of affection and weakness. There is a connection between the story and Ekwefi's courageous pursuit of Chielo to the shrine of *Agbala*, a male god. On

---

96 Osei-Nyame, Kwadwo, "Chinua Achebe Writing Culture," 155.

that infamous night, Ekwefi challenged the configurations of masculine ideology and the legitimacy of the laws of the land. She introduced a cause for renegotiation of identity and reality in the clan. Furthermore, one wonders why Okonkwo could not stop Ekwefi from following Chielo to the shrine on that fateful night, even after the priestess had warned her not to go before the mighty *Agbala*. In Umuofia, darkness held a vague terror even for the bravest of men, let alone women and children. The night Ekwefi followed Chielo to the shrine was described as 'full of thick darkness'; therefore, this implies uncommon bravery, and her journey with Chielo hints at a positive and epic heroic endeavor in which Ekwefi's bravery accords her a significant role.[97] Ekwefi was a symbol of opposition to the male-centered social order, and her bravery was more than noticed, strengthening whatever arguments there were for women to have a higher stake in the society.

According to Osei-Nyame, "Ezinma's uncompleted fable in which Yams are wrestled has the dominance of yam, the symbol of authority and power within Umuofia already under question. Ezinma's tale supplies a contrastive paradigm for questioning not only Okonkwo's authority but also the masculine traditions as a whole."[98] Again, her proposal to carry her father's chair to the clan's gathering was also symbolic, because she demanded a change in the social order of Umuofia. Any keen observer would also have noticed that the social order was tilting when, without hesitation, Ekwefi ran to bang on Okonkwo's door and woke him up when Ezinma suddenly took ill. Okonkwo would later say that Ekwefi was "the only one who would have the audacity to bang on his door." These acts by these three women, as simple as they might look, were truly courageous in the context of the time. They started the change that eventually swept through the social sphere of Umuofia. This change was already visible to Ogbuefi Ezeudu, the oldest man in the clan, who

---

97 Osei-Nyame, Kwadwo, "Chinua Achebe Writing Culture," 157.
98 Ibid, 160.

related to his visitors what his father told him about the punishment for the breaking of the clan's week of peace. He recalled that his father had told him that things were not the way they used to be in their own time.

Achebe gave women a raw deal in *Things Fall Apart*, and they vested them with the choice and responsibility of changing the narrative of male domination. They took it. The change they triggered gradually transformed the tribe, purging it of excesses and packaging it for a sophisticated world order to come. Thus, the social life of contemporary Igbos is markedly different and distant from Umuofia. The central essence of the culture remains, but what we have today is exceptionally different from the precolonial Igbo culture. The status of women has changed considerably. Today, women are able to achieve feats which were previously made for men. For instance, we have ministers, pastors, businesswomen, authors, actors, musicians, lecturers, lawyers, and many others, among Igbo women. Women have been able to attain higher positions in society.

CHAPTER IV

Interview with Chief Pete Edochie

(Okonkwo in the Movie Adaptation of *Things Fall Apart*)

on Igbo Culture and
Things Fall Apart

On the 5th of December 2019, I visited Chief Pete Edochie at his residence in Enugu (a city located in South-Eastern Nigeria). He welcomed me with warmth as he made good a pledge to grant me an interview. Enugu, by the way, is quite significant in the history of the Igbo culture, as it once was the capital city of the Igbo nation. In 1900, the Southern Nigerian Protectorate was established by the colonial administration of the British Empire and Enugu played a major role in that respect.

Chief Pete Edochie, MON, is a Nigerian actor and a renowned ambassador of Igbo culture around the globe. He is one of Africa's most talented actors, being the recipient of an *Industry Merit Award* from Africa Magic, and a Lifetime Achievement Award from the Africa Film Academy. A seasoned administrator and broadcaster, Edochie came into prominence in the 1980s when he played the lead role (Okonkwo) in an NTA (Nigerian Television Authority) adaptation of Chinua Achebe's all-time bestselling novel, *Things Fall Apart*. Edochie descends from the Igbo people of Nigeria and is a very committed Catholic. In 2003, President Olusegun Obasanjo conferred him with a national honor as a Member of the Order of the Niger (MON).[99]

On the Igbos, Origin, Culture, and Tradition

Chief Edochie, the protagonist (Okonkwo) in the movie adaptation of *Things Fall Apart*, is known for his interest in promoting the Igbo culture globally. In this regard, when asked about his take on the issue of the origin of the Igbo people and the assertion that they originated from Eri, he did not hesitate to share his knowledge of the culture with me.

QUESTION 1: According to Igbo oral tradition, and research works carried out on the Igbo culture and tradition, most scholars have come to agree that the Igbo people are descendants of *Eri*. What have you to say with respect to this?

EDOCHIE: I believe that we are descendants of *Eri*. If you go to Aguleri, to a place called *Ogbu-Gad*, you will be persuaded without too much talk that we descended from there (Eri). We are in a sense *Israelis* because most of what we do are the things they do. The way we conduct our divination when we want to contact the spirit of our ancestors is exactly how they do theirs. The practice in the Igbo culture whereby a man marries the widow of his brother originated from there. Circumcision after eight days also originated from there, and these are the things that we alone do. Even the Igbo name 'Ada', is also what they call their first daughter, so we have many things in common. It is not an accident, except that sometimes, chronicles of

---

99 "Pete Edochie," Wikipedia, last edited on 6 March, 2023, https://en.wikipedia.org/wiki/Pete_Edochie.

our history fail to acknowledge most of these things because they do not research properly.

Igbo people have a lot of problems; every person wants to claim that the others originated from his own particular place. If you go to Arochukwu you will be told that the Aro man fell from the sky and other similar stories. So, I am of the opinion and may go along with the product of that research that we are all descendants of Eri, and Eri is one of the sons of Gad, so that explains aspects of our culture that are akin to those of the Jews.

QUESTION 2: Can you give any examples of some of the aspects that distinguished the Igbo tradition from others?

EDOCHIE: An example is the use of *Nzu* (white chalk) and kola nuts among the Igbo. "If you look around here, you will see that wooden saucer there on my table; it is for kola nut. Then there is that large chunk of white chalk there; it means a lot in Igbo land: If a visitor should come to see me, I will give him kola nut, it means 'welcome'. Then I will ask him to take part of the white chalk, which he can paste anywhere, and mark some on the ground. It is an indication that he went to a man's house. Now, what does that *Nzu* signify? In those days when we heard of a lot of kidnapping as some aspect of our culture, people disappeared if we couldn't identify where they were coming from, but if you visit a man and he offers you *Nzu*, you mark it around your eye, either the left or the right, your stomach, etc. The moment you step out people will look at you and know that you are from somebody's place, and they will not touch nor harm you. That is the origin of that aspect of the culture that a lot of people do not know. The Igbo culture is beautiful and fantastic.

One other important aspect of our culture is the meaning behind our religious and traditional use of kola nut and its significance in the Igbo culture. It is only the Igbo man that picks up kola nut and prays with it. In picking up a kola nut, he reminds God of their covenant: 'you created us and we are here to worship you to glorify your name.' That is the essence of our traditional kola nut ritual, the presentation, and offering of kola nut in any Igbo gathering. Hence, in picking up kola nut the Igbo man prays with these words: 'O Lord, we thank you for today, we seek for your peace and love and beg for progress. This is why each time we are doing it, praying with kola nut, we are reminding ourselves of the fact that 'God created us to know him, love him and to serve him in this world, and to be happy with him forever in the next.'

When we pray with the kola nut, we are constantly reminding ourselves that one day someday, we will be granted the beatific vision if we have lived well on earth. That is the essence of the Igbo traditional use of kola nut in their social gathering. The white man knows little or nothing about our culture, but then he wants to assess us with his own barometer, which is very wrong. For instance, the Igbo man knows why he offers kola nut, his covenant with God, but the white man does not offer kola nut, he does not know what it means. Therefore, he is not in a position to condemn it. In offering kola nut, we take a little piece and drop it on the ground for our ancestors. That little piece shows that you are aware that our ancestors still exist and that they are interceding for us before God. It is the same thing we do in the Catholic Church; you will not be a saint while you are still alive. If you lead a pious life while you are alive, your name will be used for prayers. If those prayers are answered and miracles are obtained, you are on your way to sainthood. Therefore, what the Igbo do by recognizing that those who are dead have gone to intercede for us is precisely what the Catholic Church is doing, but those who do not understand it will think you are being fetish.

The white man wanted to use his own beliefs to supplant ours, but we resisted. We believe that there is a Supreme Being who created us, and how we relate to this Being is by showing appreciation and offering our gratitude for the bounteousness of nature, and what he has given to us. And how do we do it? If we do it through a human being, he is corruptible, so you carve something that looks like a human being; it does not talk, it does not see and it does not breathe. It is inanimate. Therefore, it is incorruptible and we agree that this is where we are going to meet. This incorruptible material will take all the products from our farm to God to show our appreciation. That is the origin of *Arusi*, the Igbo carved wood, representing man for its incorruptibility. Then the collective will of the people is used to invigorate that carving and that is why it commands spiritual potency because the will of the people has been invested in it, and anybody who goes contrary to the will of the people will now be punished. This is spiritualism. Hence, the Igbo culture does not worship idols, this is their way of getting to God and this is why it has been working. If you ask people to swear by *Arusi* they will be afraid because if they go contrary to it, it will kill them. All power comes from God, and everything depends on how we decide to approach Him. Some decided to approach Him through other 'gods'. For instance, there is a native doctor in my place, somebody went to see him one day and saw the photograph of Blessed Michael Iwene Tansi (an honored Catholic priest) where he kept all his *Arusi* and other things. He asked the native doctor what the picture was doing there and the native doctor laughed and said that Tansi was their '*Nwadiala*' (kinsman), because Tansi's mother came from his place. And he further said: look, these things he does for you people, he also does it for us too when we beg him. This explains a lot about the Igbo religion; the native doctor had all his effigies there, but then, there was also the photograph of Blessed Tansi there. So, when the native doctor gets to talk, he remembers that Tansi is also one of his ancestors and so will implore his intercession too. This is our culture. It is not fetish. Look at it from this perspective, the native doctor had the courage to say 'whatever he does for you, he also does for us.' And, you may not believe it, but through their invocations, Tansi has converted and done a lot in our area. Therefore, when the white man turns around and employs terms that tend to discredit us and our mode of worship, I think he is being uncharitable.

Considering the inevitable evolution of cultures in contact with other cultures, it is obvious that in today's Igbo society, *Nzu*, the white chalk, is no longer in use like in the early Igbo society.

QUESTION 3: How can you describe the meeting between the two cultures, that is, the British and the Igbo culture?

EDOCHIE: Culture is eclectic. It means that you borrow from so many sources so that you can update your own culture, in order to facilitate communion with others. Now, out of ignorance, we were killing twins, and doing other such things. For example, if a woman sprouted hairs on her chest she was rejected by the men; if a child came out feet first from the mother's womb, it was seen as an abomination, etc. These things were alien to us, but the white man came and taught us that there was nothing unusual about these things. So, there was no need to discriminate against such people or cast them away to the evil forest to die, no. However, in learning these things we were not supposed to cede our entire culture to the white man. What he wanted to do was to supplant ours completely. People have their mannerisms, in terms of food, people have their alimentary preferences, and so on. For instance, our Lord Jesus Christ took 'bread and wine' to present Himself to his disciples. If He had been born in Enugu State in Nigeria, he would have taken '*Okpa* and Palm wine' to do so. That is it. You get attuned to a particular place in life. The white man has his own way of life, and we have ours too. We can borrow from him, let him borrow from us too.

On the other hand, the white man's culture also left a negative impact on ours. One thing to consider is this: the white man does not know the values of marriage; we shall teach him that. The Igbo culture has marital values and that is why you hardly hear of divorce in our culture. Sadly, today most of our women have come to embrace all that nonsense, and you can now hear of such things as divorce and other things in marriage. Considerably, things keep changing in our present-day society, like in every other human society. No condition is static in life. We try to preserve our values, but we also try to update them so that when we find ourselves in the midst of people who are not products of our culture we can still relate with them. In our culture, we pay reverence to God. Let us see it this way, I am a Catholic; when I get into the Church, I genuflect in acknowledgment of the existence of the superior spiritual being in whose presence I find myself. That is why I genuflect. Now, it is madness to genuflect before a woman because I want to give her a ring. In Igbo land, if you genuflect before a woman, you have conceded all your authority to her. That is the white man's culture and most contemporary Igbos are embracing this aspect, which is not in any way our lifestyle. In our culture, it is the woman who, during the traditional marriage, presents her husband to her family by kneeling before him with a cup of palm wine in her hands. This act simply signifies that the man has been accepted as the husband of the woman. It is the woman who kneels before the husband, not vice versa.

Title Taking

QUESTION 4: Why is title taking so important among Igbo people?

EDOCHIE: It shows your position in the traditional Igbo society. When you take a title, you wear a Red Cap and there are things you are forbidden to do. There are aspects of our culture you must defend stoutly. That is the essence of taking titles in Igboland. If there is any pockmark or something suspicious about your background and origin, you are not given a title. I was not given a title because I am a very huge man; my achievements were assessed with traditional barometers in our culture and I was found to have qualified. This is why I have many titles (like *Ononenyi n'ntege, Agaba idu* of Aguleri, MON — a national honor from the Nigerian Government, Grand Patron of the Basilica in Onitsha and one of the protagonists for the canonization of Blessed Iwene Tansi, etc.). On the other hand, looking at the situation in contemporary Igbo society, there are now possibilities of acquiring titles with money. Some people now take titles not because they merited them but because they have made money. There are always two sides to every coin. There were people who belonged to dynasties, and in dynasties, succession is by primogeniture, the first person takes over. Now, people made money and decided that these things (kingship) should be rotated, and that was what contaminated this aspect of the traditional value. Most of those who were custodians of the culture traditionally and who became kings were not educated. Now, most young men have acquired advanced education and want to contest traditional stools in their various locations. In some sense, it is good because education is the key to everything. But the inherent danger is that the moment you plug money into something like that, the values are desecrated and that is what is happening today. But we shall not allow that aspect to die."

Things Fall Apart

QUESTION 5: As the main character of the film, *Things Fall Apart*, do you think Achebe's aim was to represent the Igbo traditions and culture, which he felt had been overlooked by the western writers? What could probably be his aim in *Things Fall Apart*?

EDOCHIE: The invasion of the culture of the people and the resistance that the people offered, that is what *Things Fall Apart* is all about. In my place, we value honor a great deal. Rather than for a man to remain alive and witness shame, he will prefer to die. Which was precisely what Okonkwo did. He resisted the white man. Okonkwo was born at a time when our culture was being invaded; there was this onrushing of a wild culture and so, there was a clash. And when both cultures clashed, there were deaths here and there. Okonkwo was conservative. He wanted to ensure that the essence, the core, of his own culture was preserved. Whereas the colonists were intent on ensuring that they forced their own culture on us, and that was how the clash came about. So, what Achebe did was to mirror that situation perfectly, and it worked because the book has been translated into 53 languages, and that's an indication that it was welcomed all over the world.

QUESTION 6: How did you feel playing Okonkwo in the movie, *Things Fall Apart?*

EDOCHIE: When I finished playing the role of Okonkwo, the BBC watched it, flew in to interview me, and went and interviewed Chinua Achebe. Achebe, in his interview with the BBC, said Pete Edochie gave it the best interpretation ever. So, to this day, I am called *Ebubedike* for it in Igboland. It was a very successful portrayal of our culture and it showed the pride of the Igbo man. The Igbo man is proud of his culture, and he is fulfilling some essence of existence that must be emulated by other people. The Igbo man is very creative, always obsessed with the desire to conquer his environment. He does not believe that the environment offers challenges that are insurmountable. The indomitable spirit of the Igbo man is what attracts jealousy from the other tribes today because wherever the Igbo man finds himself, he makes a home out of that place (and that is precisely what the Jews do), and there is absolutely nothing anybody can do about it. In Igboland we call it *onatarachi,* if the good Lord gives something to you, it is congenital, there is absolutely nothing anybody can do about it. The most people can do is to be jealous of you, but they cannot destroy what God has given you.

Therefore, what Achebe did was a very successful portrayal of what the Igbo man represents when it comes to defending his culture.

QUESTION 7: Some scholars have argued that *Things Fall Apart* is somewhat the tragedy of Okonkwo. For them, Okonkwo's death was actually the collapse and death of the Igbo culture and tradition. What do you think? What can you say regarding the post-colonial state of the Igbo culture, which in many ways reflects itself in contemporary Igbo society?

EDOCHIE: Firstly, Okonkwo's death is not a tragedy. What is the perspective from which they are assessing Okonkwo, and the resistance he offered to the invasion of his culture? If you read *Henry VI* by Williams Shakespeare, there are aspects where he says: 'If it be a crime to value honor, then I am the most offending slave alive.' I always like to refer to that bit because that is what propels me in life. I do not joke with my honor. It does not make me a perfect person, but I insist on projecting moral rectitude because many people look up to me for inspiration, for guidance. Okonkwo, I said earlier found himself in a situation where he had to represent a conflict. This is Igbo culture represented by Okonkwo; now, there is this onrush of white culture and Okonkwo wanted to ensure that our own culture was preserved. We wouldn't mind existing side by side with whatever the white man represented, but the white man wanted to ensure that he supplanted our own culture, and this is what Okonkwo resisted. So, his life was not a tragedy; anybody viewing it from that point is mistaken. Again, it did not in any way signal the collapse of our tradition, no. On the contrary, it reinforced our conviction in our traditional values. Hence, Okonkwo is not in any way a failure, and his self-sacrifice was not a tragedy; he was willing to die for what he believed in and that is honor. It should be seen from that perspective. Okonkwo was a concept. Like I said earlier, *Things Fall Apart*, essentially, was a conflict between a new order represented by the white man, the imperialist, and our culture, represented by Okonkwo. Now, Okonkwo wanted to preserve the essence, the sacrosanctity of our own culture. The white man was out there to use his own culture and whatever he represented to supplant ours, and Okonkwo resisted it. Okonkwo was a hero; he was not a failure.

I am somebody who will not compromise values for anything. I am a titled person, and that is what Okonkwo represents for the Igbo man. Today many people see me as the cultural ambassador of the Igbo nation and I am proud to be referred to as such. I am a happy Igbo man. After I did *Things Fall Apart*, I received calls from all over the world. Whom do I represent? The Igbo race, of course, and I am proud to be an Igbo man.

As I said earlier, culture is eclectic. That means that there is an inherent dynamism in culture. You borrow from a couple of sources to reinforce the essence of your own culture, to facilitate communion with other cultures. Now, what our people do is they give up on our own culture and then embrace the white man's culture. This is stupid in a way. When I was growing up, I bore a lot of foreign names. People saw me as epitomizing the movie industry even before its birth in Nigeria. As I grew older, I got more involved with our culture and came to appreciate its beauty.

In *Things Fall Apart*, Okonkwo was not a failure; he represented the resistance of the Igbo man against the invasion of his culture by foreign values. It is the most successful book ever written on the continent of Africa, and this is why it has been translated into many languages worldwide. And I say this with an authority that nobody can challenge. The book gained popularity worldwide because of its content, because of what it represents. Okonkwo was a human being in the production, but he was more or less a concept. In the film, wherever Igbo people were, they were represented in that production, (including the *Ikwerre* people and those in the Delta area). Therefore, *Things Fall Apart* has very easily been the most successful book ever written on the continent and I am proud to have played it. I am happy that Chinua who wrote the book said I gave it the interpretation after his heart and was calling me Okonkwo until he died. Agreeably, Okonkwo was not conceived as a failure, he was projected as the black man's epic resistance to the invasion of his culture by white values.

QUESTION 8: It has been argued by some scholars that Okonkwo's death is a signal of how close the Igbo culture is with respect to the western cultures. What do you have to say in this regard?

EDOCHIE: No one on earth can educate me on my culture; no white man can! On the contrary, I am superior to the white man in the sense that I am employing his own language fluently to communicate with him whereas he cannot speak my own language. I was trained formally as a broadcaster in the BBC. Now, one of our lecturers one day called me and said, 'Pete, I am not ashamed to say this, I am an Englishman, but you have more English in your head than I do. You communicate so effectively in my own language in a capacity I cannot boast of; how did you do it? And I said I don't know how I did it. Now, the white people I find myself in their midst respected me a great deal because of my part of communication. Right from the era of colonization, the white man had this acerbic view of our own culture, which for me, is regrettable in a way. Charles Darwin talked about the evolution of man, and he contended that human beings evolved from animals. Bernard Shaw took him up on it and said that if people evolved from monkeys, why are there still monkeys today? Why haven't the monkeys devolved? What the white man does not want to accept is that renowned archaeologists have proven that Africa is the original home of man and, therefore, he is not happy to acknowledge an African's superiority in various aspects. He wants to keep cowing you because he came with his bible and all… the time is gone for all that. Hence, Okonkwo's death did not in any way project that the Igbo culture is not open to change.

Looking at the present-day Igbo society, one could without doubt, acknowledge the degree of change that had occurred in the social life of the Igbos. Considerably, the Igbo people are one of the most open-minded people on the African continent, and enculturation has done a great deal in the community's social life.

The white man said we sold our brothers into slavery, and that is fallacy. He came with preconceived ideas to come and take away our people; we did not go to them neither did we invite them. The white man is not in a position to appreciate the cultural representation we had in *Things Fall Apart*. He does not understand it. We have honour; in my own area of Igbo land you will be told that it is better to die rather than be alive and witness shame. And people are still doing it till tomorrow. We do not believe in struggling too much for what belongs to other people, God has given us something, a lot of it.

On Gender

QUESTION 9: In the Igbo tradition represented by Achebe in *Things Fall Apart,* women were not represented in most areas like in the title system, clan gathering, etc. They were not part of the secret societies (*Egwugwu*, etc.), and they were not given the right to say or do certain things that were exclusively reserved for men. Why do we have such a representation of the Igbo culture that appears to show little importance to women?

EDOCHIE: Man is the head of the family in Igboland. Some of the white man's culture constitutes anathema in Igbo culture. The white man's culture tolerates marriages without children, while the Igbo culture slightly does not. For the Igbos, marriages are meant to be procreative and children are the precious fruits of this union. The white man subjected himself lavishly to the whims of women, whereas the Igbo culture believes in nurturing women by grooming them into what society expected of them. I have lived with my wife for 50 years and we are going to be 51 soon. Nobody has ever come into this place and said 'Pete please stop beating this woman, you will kill her'. I never saw my father beat my mother. Therefore, I cannot touch my wife. It is a tradition. I have five sons, all married, with thirteen grandchildren. None of my sons has ever struck their wife, and it will not happen because they never saw me beat their mother. So, that's what we call the preservation of our culture, the essence of our culture. The white man's culture is very different from the Igbo culture. For instance, a white man meets you, falls in love with you, and marries you in one town, but before you get to the other town, you are separated again. It doesn't mean much to him. For the Igbo man, there is something sacrosanct about marriage, which he is compelled to preserve. He swore before God to be attached to this woman, and he does everything he can to ensure that that woman does not regret being married to him, whatever it is she requires, he must make sure he provides it.

In our culture, women are not being discriminated against because of their gender, no. The issue is that women are given out in marriage to other cultures. Therefore, they cannot be good representatives of their own culture where they were born into, and for this reason, the man is the head of the family. There are many things the white man does which constitute anathema in our culture. The western culture voluntarily promotes marriages without children, while there is no such thing in our culture. When my mother got married to my father, she was told by her parents to go and have children with my father. My mother came knowing fully well that that was her marital commitment to their union. Our culture was intended to protect women, to preserve their place in society. I have to provide for my wife whatever the society requires of her because she is carrying my name. Before an Igbo man gets married, questions are asked, there is a middleman, and questions about the longevity and background of the person's family are asked. These things are necessary because they constitute the values on which our culture is planted. It is considered that if a woman couldn't live with her husband, it will be a risk for a man to go and marry from that family because her daughter will behave like she did. In our culture, there is a situation where a woman marries a fellow woman. There is normally no male in the family, they are all females and so there is always one female to be left there. And they will go and get a young girl and keep her in the house so that she can breed and get boys, so that can perpetuate that lineage instead of allowing it to die. On the other hand, in western culture, if a man gets one daughter, he is satisfied; that is not our culture. If you don't have a man to represent your lineage and perpetuate it you keep trying. If it means marrying from elsewhere, you do so; because it's your name and it's our culture. Hence, the Igbo man gets married to his wife in order to protect her.

Africa is the original home of man, and we have our set of values. It is not gender discrimination. For instance, we don't allot land to our women to build house for one reason; it may happen that she goes and gets married to a Lebanese or someone from another country tomorrow without knowing anything about the culture. In Igbo culture, we don't want that kind of contamination. This was why, in the past, when a man died, the brother was persuaded to marry the wife so that the blood was not contaminated. In our culture, one man does not marry a woman. This is it: I get married to a woman, when my relations come, the question they will ask is "where is 'our' wife?" and not "where is 'your' wife?" My relations will take her as part of them and will protect her in every occasion. The Igbo people have a proverbial hospitality, it is like asking: do you know this man? He is our relation, and therefore he is welcomed. I was trained in the white man's society; I love the white man, I don't hate him. But, let him appreciate me. This is where I am coming from; he has no right to inflict his culture on me and enslave my mentality permanently; he is not allowed to do that.

Women are not leaders in Igbo society and there is no way the queen could have been a king in Igbo culture. No matter her talent, she will get married and her husband will become the king if there is no successor from their lineage. From my own perspective, it is not gender discrimination. It is a very well organized, civilized society. A society that runs on norms that reflect our nature as human beings and not as automatons or machines.

———

I would like to acknowledge Edochie's explanation of the Igbo use of kola nut when he said that "In offering kola nut, we take a little piece and drop it on the ground for our ancestors. That little piece shows that you are aware that our ancestors still exist and that they are interceding for us before God. It is the same thing we do in the Catholic Church; you will not be a saint while you are still alive. If you lead a pious life while you are alive, your name will be used for prayers." Every culture has one or two things in common. It depends on how they are viewed and on how cultures are able to look beyond themselves to acknowledge the worth of the other. No culture has it all good and the other bad. If we look closely at other cultures, we definitely might see a sort of resemblance or something shared in common. We will discover that different group of people sometimes share the same value and same belief but the difference is only on how these values and beliefs are carried out by each of them.

Again, I must agree with Edochie that culture is eclectic. The belief that cultures evolve from a 'primitive culture' to form part of a 'global culture,' be it pacifically as a result of enculturation or through a series of clashes with other cultures, is never to be underestimated.

For example, in *Things Fall Apart,* Okonkwo's exile to Mbanta marked the passage or the evolution of the culture of Umuofia to a new and global one. As we read in the first paragraph of chapter twenty, "seven years was a long time to be away from one's clan. A man's place was not always there waiting for him. As soon as he left, someone else rose and filled it. The clan was like a lizard, if it lost its tail it soon grew another." This can be attributed to every culture. Culture is not rigid and firmly in one place. Like a lizard, it grows a new tail once the old one is lost. It could be said, as it is with any national constitution, that cultures are always in the process of revision and amendment. Revisions are made by changing or modifying those aspects or particularities that no longer fit into the new and desired order to adapt to the global culture. Culture is not stagnant as we can detect from the hint that "a man's place was not always there, waiting for him." Life moves on with its changes. This was the case of Umuofia; seven years were enough to incur a reasonable transformation. We were told that Okonkwo, on his arrival in Umuofia after seven years of exile, was unable to recognize that that was the warrior clan he left a few years ago. Whatever may be the reason, one thing noteworthy is that his clan was no longer the way it used to be. The missionaries had now settled in their land, and his clan members gradually became acquainted with them. He had lost his place as one of the lords of the clan, "he has lost the chance to lead his warlike clan against the new religion, which, he was told, had gained ground. He had lost the years in which he might have taken the highest titles in the clan. But some of these losses were not irreparable." One crucial thing was that the clan suffered losses, of which some were reparable; the clan was not completely devastated. For people to regain their real self, they must get rid of their unreal self. This is clear in the case of Umuofia, which had to get rid of its old self with regard to customs like the killing of twins, human sacrifice, casting away of members into the evil forest, etc., to regain its new self.

Part two of *Things Fall Apart* marked the beginning of Umuofia's new self. Okonkwo's exile was very significant in the history of Umuofia as well as in his own life. Umuofia turned a new leaf in his absence. In a way, it could probably be said that Okonkwo's demise started at the end of the first part when he had to leave Umuofia for Mbanta. He described it as being cast out of the clan "like a fish onto a dry, sandy beach." A fish out of water has no life, and that was what Okonkwo's life appeared to be in exile. His many life aspirations and his passion for becoming one of the greatest and most revered men of the clan were shattered when he left the land. He became voiceless and powerless, both in Umuofia and in Mbanta, for he could neither interfere in the social life of Mbanta, as he was not part of the clan, nor could he interfere in that of his clan, because he was banished into exile for many years.

Conclusion

Things Fall Apart demonstrated that the displacement of Okonkwo and the unjust imposition of the presumed developed culture over the presumed undeveloped culture was only an indication of the developed culture's uncivilized way of taking advantage of the 'presumed inferior culture.' The colonial government's superiority complex led it to over-step its boundaries in Umuofia in the sense that the empire, finding itself out of place, displaced the owner of the land, and this notwithstanding, was on the verge of promulgating its insensitivity on its so-called *Pacification of the Primitive Tribes of the Lower Niger.* Achebe frowned at the barbarous acts of the District Commissioner towards the end of the novel, and demonstrated that the Igbos, and Africa as a whole, had cultures and traditions, were civilized, and were sensitive to the wickedness of the District Commissioner. Additionally, he captured the difficulties of those living within a time and place of diverse cultures. At such times, cultures and societies are, in the worst-case scenario, on the verge of extinction and, in the best-case scenario, on the verge of transformation and renewal. In the case of Umuofia, despite the rivalry between the two cultures, clansmen lived in a time of cultural diversity and were driven to preserve their identity while being enticed by the missionaries' particular educational offer. At the end of the day, there were ample choices for both parties, especially for the culture on the receiving end of an invading culture. It had the power to choose if and how to fight the multiple essences of colonization. In the case of Achebe and his protagonist, Okonkwo, Begam's position holds enormous weight. He posits that if forerunners like Okonkwo and his likes "have been vanquished wrestling the demons of multiplicity, Achebe has emerged from these spiritual contests with a deeper and more comprehensive sense of what it means to inhabit the alternate worlds of post-colonialism, worlds that are at once aristocratic and democratic, heroic and ironic, ancient and contemporary." (Begam, 1997).

Therefore, Achebe's survival of the colonial conquest and his subsequent rise to prominence with a heartening history of the Igbo people lend credibility to his narrative in *Things Fall Apart.*

Bibliography

1. Achebe, Chinua. *The African Trilogy, Things Fall Apart, Everyman's Library, Alfred A. Knopf, New York, London, Toronto, 2010.*
2. Achebe, Chinua, Killam, G.D. "The role of a writer in a new nation." *African writers on African writing,* (1973): 7-13.
3. Achebe, Chinua. "An Image of Africa." In *Heart of Darkness.* Ed. Paul B. Armstrong, 306-319. London: W. W. Norton and Co., 2017.
4. Afigbo, Adiele E. *Ropes of sand.* Oxford university press, 1981.
5. Ayeleru, Babatunde. "Where is the Text? Chinua Achebe's *Things Fall Apart." Spheres Public and Private: Western Genres in African Literature,* ed. Gordon Collier, Matatu 39, Amsterdam & New York: Editions Rodopi, (2011). 273-282.
6. Basden, George T., *Among the Ibos of Nigeria,* London: Seley, Service and Co. Limited, 1921.
7. Beckham, Jack M. "Achebe's *Things fall apart." The Explicator.* Vol. 60(4) (2002): 229-231.
8. Begam, Richard. "Achebe's sense of an ending: History and tragedy in *Things Fall Apart." Studies in the Novel,* 29, no. 3 (Fall 1997): 396-411.
9. Bekler, Ecevit, "The true face of pre.colonial Africa in *Things Fall Apart," Respectus Philologicus, Vol.25, no. 30 (2014):* 96-98.
10. Borman, David. "Playful Ethnography: Chinua Achebe's Things Fall Apart and Nigerian Education." *Ariel: A review of international English literature,* Johns Hopkins University Press. Vol. 46 No. 3 (2015): 91-112.

11. Chukwuelobe, Matthew C. "Language and Igbo Philosophy." *Philosophy Today*, Vol.39 (Spring 1995): 25-30.

12. Dannenberg, Hilary. "The many voices of *Things Fall Apart*", *Interventions*, Vol. 11(2) (2009): 176-179

13. Diana, Akers Rhoads. "Culture in Chinua Achebe's *Things Fall Apart*". *African Studies Review*, Vol. 36, No. 2 (Sep.1993): 61-72.

14. Dr. Pona Mahanta, Retd., Dibakar Maut. "Impact of Colonizer on the Colonized: A Postcolonial Study of Nigerian Igbo Culture and History in Chinua Achebe's *Things Fall Apart*." *IOSR Journal of Humanities and Social Science*. Vol.19, Issue 11, Ver. II (Nov. 2014): 01-08.

15. Equiano, Olaudah, *Olaudah Equiano or Gustavus Vassa, the African*, Vol. 1(London: T. Wilkins, 1789).

16. Edochie, Pete, "On Igbo Culture and *Things Fall Apart*", interview by Emmanuela C. Nwokeke CP., Enugu, December 5, 2019.

17. Ezekwugo, C.M. *Ora-Eri Nnokwa and Nri Dynasty*. (Enugu: Lengon Printers,1987).

18. Gikandi, Simon. "Chinua Achebe and the Invention of African Culture." *Research in African Literatures*. Vol. 32, no. 3, (Autumn, 2001): 3-8.

19. Greenberg, Jonathan, "Okonkwo and the Storyteller: Death, Accident, and Meaning in Chinua Achebe and Walter Benjamin." Montclair State University, (2007): 1-29.

20. Hoegberg, David. "Principle and Practice: The Logic of Cultural Violence in Achebe's *Things Fall Apart*". *College Literature*. Vol. 26, no. 1 (Winter 1999): 69-79.

21. Kanayo L. Nwadialor & Ikenna L. Umeanolue. "Missionary factor in the making of a Modern Igbo Nation. 1841-1940: A Historical Discourse." *Sociology*. (2012): 112-127.

22. Kenalemang, Lame Maatla. "*Things Fall Apart*: An Analysis of Pre and Post-Colonial Igbo Society." Bachelor's degree thesis, Karlstad University, 2013.

23. Korang, Kwaku Larbi. "Making a Post-Eurocentric Humanity: Tragedy, Realism, and *Things Fall Apart.*" *Research in African Literatures*, Vol. 42, No. 2 (Summer 2011): 1-29.

24. Linn Watts, Jarica. "He does not understand our customs": Narrating orality and empire in Chinua Achebe's *Things Fall Apart*". Journal of Postcolonial Writing. Vol. 46, no. 1, (February 2010): 65—75.

25. Mackenzie, Clayton G. "The Metamorphosis of Piety in Chinua Achebe's *Things Fall Apart*". *Research in African Literatures*. Vol. 27, no.2 (Summer, 1996): 128-138.

26. Mahanta Pona, Maut Dibakar. "The Impact of Colonizer on the Colonized: A Postcolonial Study of Nigerian Igbo Culture and History in Chinua Achebe's *Things Fall Apart.*" *IOSR Journal of Humanities and Social Science*, Vol. 19, no.11 (Nov.2014), 4.

27. Mirmotahari, Emad. "History as project and source in Achebe's *Things Fall Apart*". *Postcolonial Studies*, Vol. 14, no. 4 (2011): 373-385.

28. Njoku, Ndu Life; Ihenacho, Chijioke L; Onyekwelibe, James C. "The Encounter with 'Evil Forests' in Igbo-land." *Journal of Social History*. Vol.50 no.3 (2017): 466-480.

29. Ohadike, C. Don. "Igbo Culture and History." In *Things Fall Apart*. XIX-XLIX, Ibadan: Heinemann, African writers' series, 1996.

30. Okpala, Jude Chudi. "Igbo Metaphysics in Chinua Achebe's *Things Fall Apart*". Callaloo Vol. 25, no. 2 (Spring, 2002): 559—566.

31. Okwu, Augustine S. O. *Igbo Culture and the Christian Missions 1857-1957*. New York: University Press of America, 2010. (60)

32. Osei-Nyame, Kwadwo. "Chinua Achebe Writing Culture: Representations of Gender and Tradition in *Things Fall Apart.*" *Research in African Literatures*. Vol.30, no.2, (Summer, 1999): 148-164.

33. Paul B. Armstrong, ed., *Heart of Darkness*, London: W. W. Norton and Co., 2017.

34. Phillips, Ann. *The Enigma of Colonialism: British Policy in West Africa*. London: Indiana University Press and James Currey, 1989.

35. Pope Benedict XV, Encyclical on the Propagation of the Faith throughout the World, *Maximum Illud* (30 November 1919) § 11, at The Holy See, https://www.vatican.va/content/benedict-xv/en/apost_letters/documents/hf_ben-xv_apl_19191130_maximum-illud.html.

36. Pope Pius XI, Encyclical on Catholic Missions, *Rerum Ecclesiae* (28 February 1926) §1, at The Holy See, https://www.vatican.va/content/pius-xi/en/encyclicals/documents/hf_p-xi_enc_28021926_rerum-ecclesiae.html.

37. Pius XII, Encyclical on the Promotion of Catholic Missions, *Evangelii Praecones* (2 June 1951) § 2,3, at The Holy See, https://www.vatican.va/content/pius-xii/en/encyclicals/documents/hf_p-xii_enc_02061951_evangelii-praecones.html.

38. Said, Edward W. *Culture and imperialism*. London: Chatto and Windus, 1993.

39. Said, Edward W. "Yeats and Decolonization." *Nationalism, Colonialism, and Literature,* NED — University of Minnesota Press, (1990): 69—96.

40. Searle, Alison. "The Role of Missions in *Things Fall Apart* and *Nervous Conditions*". *Literature & Theology*, Vol. 21, No. 1, (March 2007): 49-65.

41. Wikipedia, "Pete Edochie," last edited on 6 March, 2023, https://en.wikipedia.org/wiki/Pete_Edochie.

www.ingramcontent.com/pod-product-compliance
Lightning Source LLC
Chambersburg PA
CBHW071121090426
42736CB00012B/1974